RELAXING COLORING BOOK FOR ADULTS

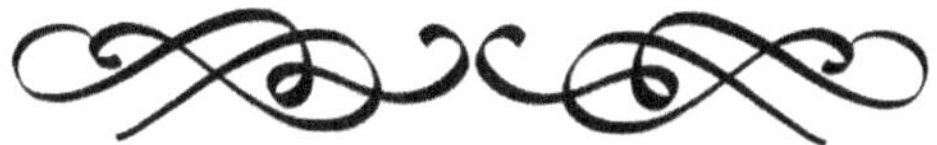

This Coloring Book Belongs To:

____

____

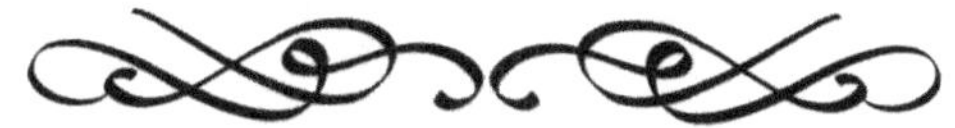

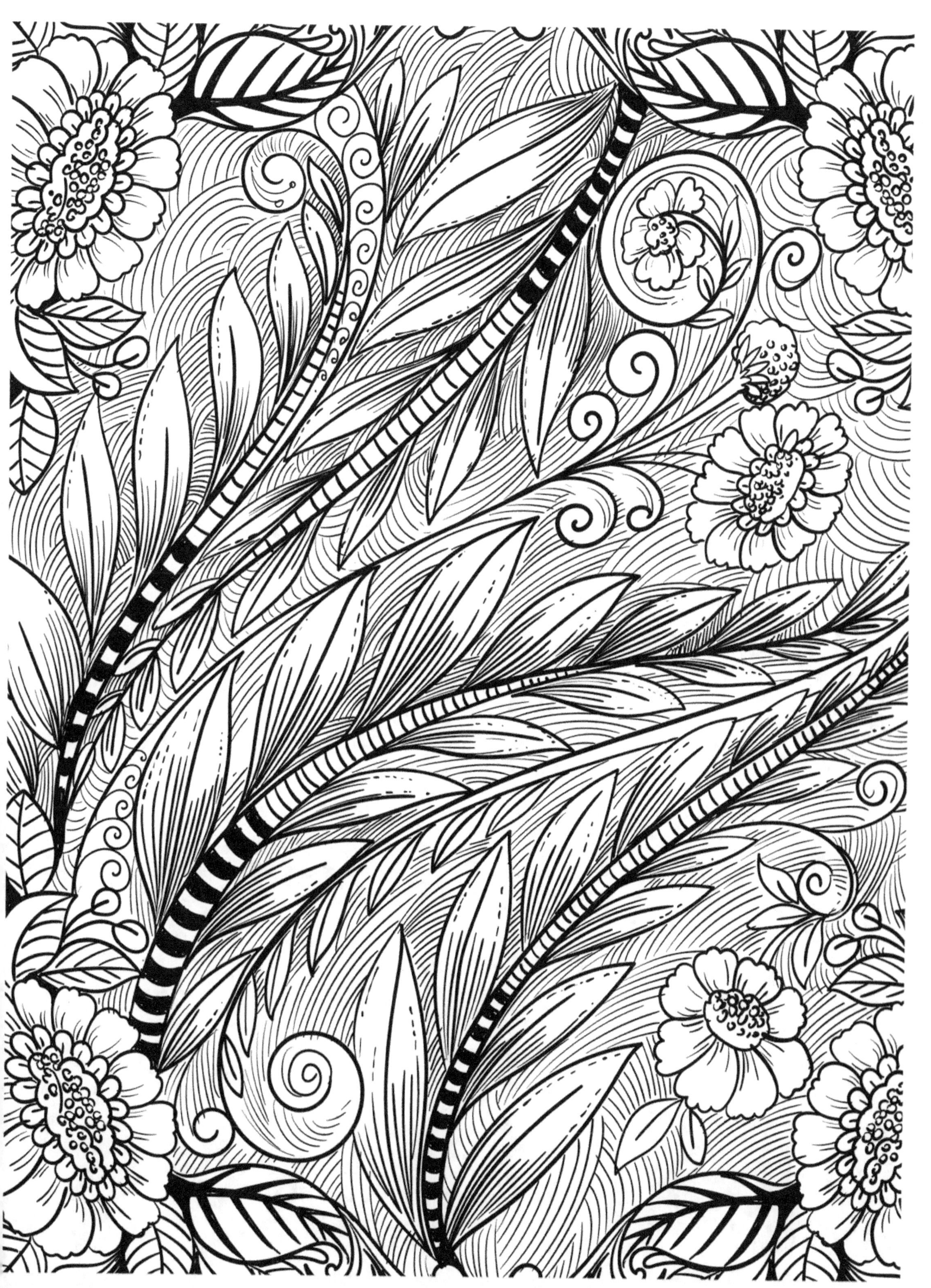

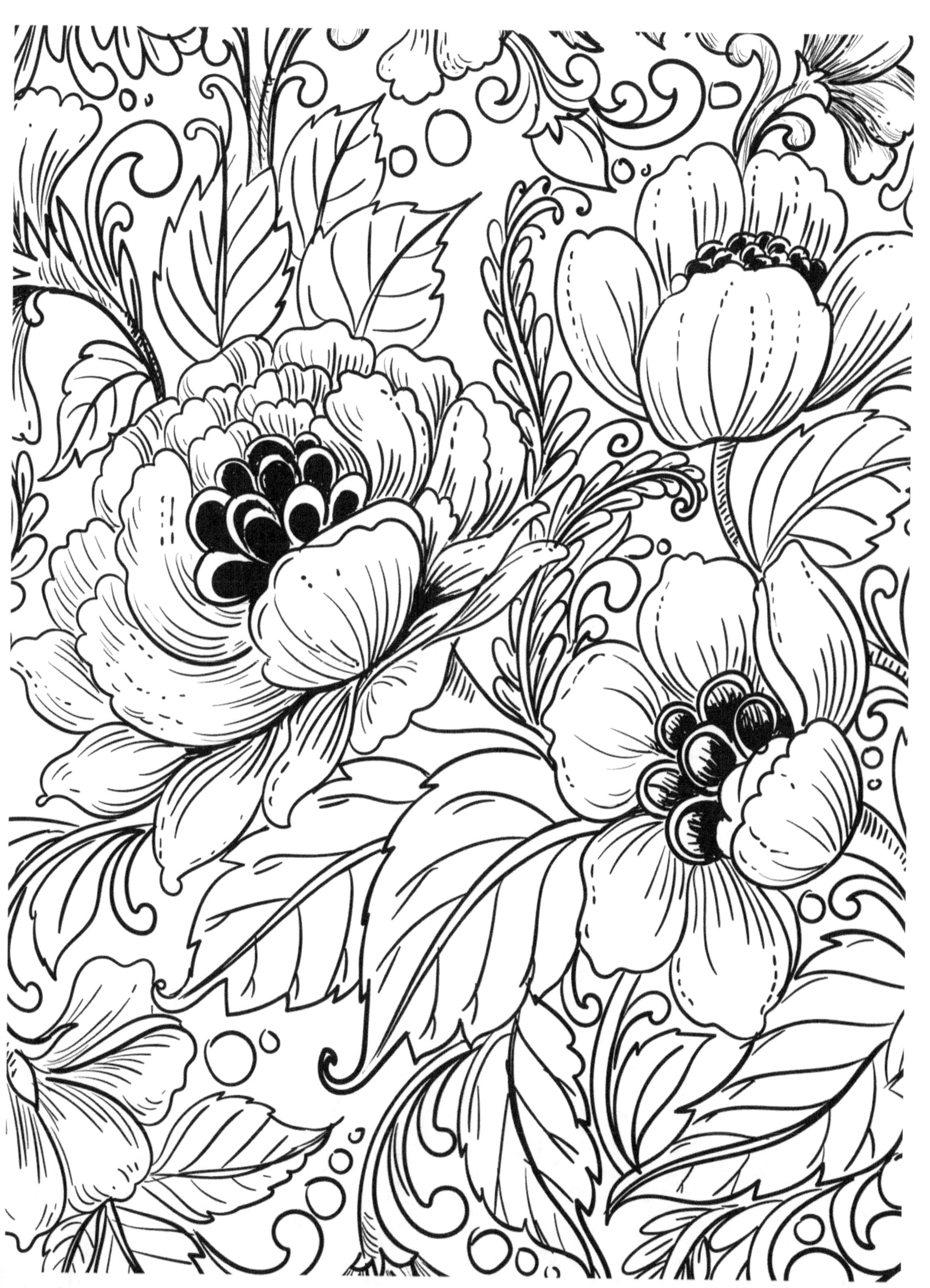

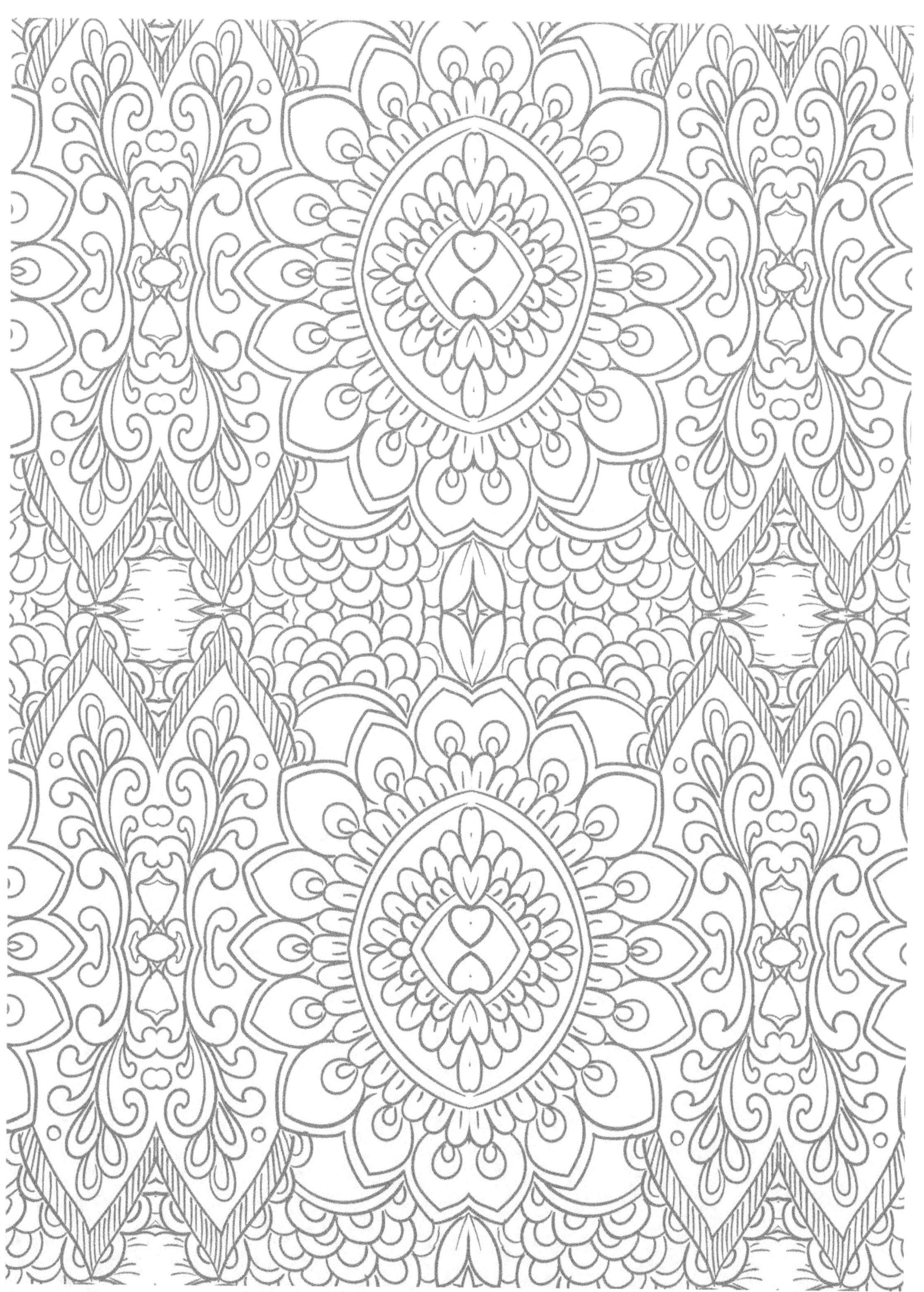

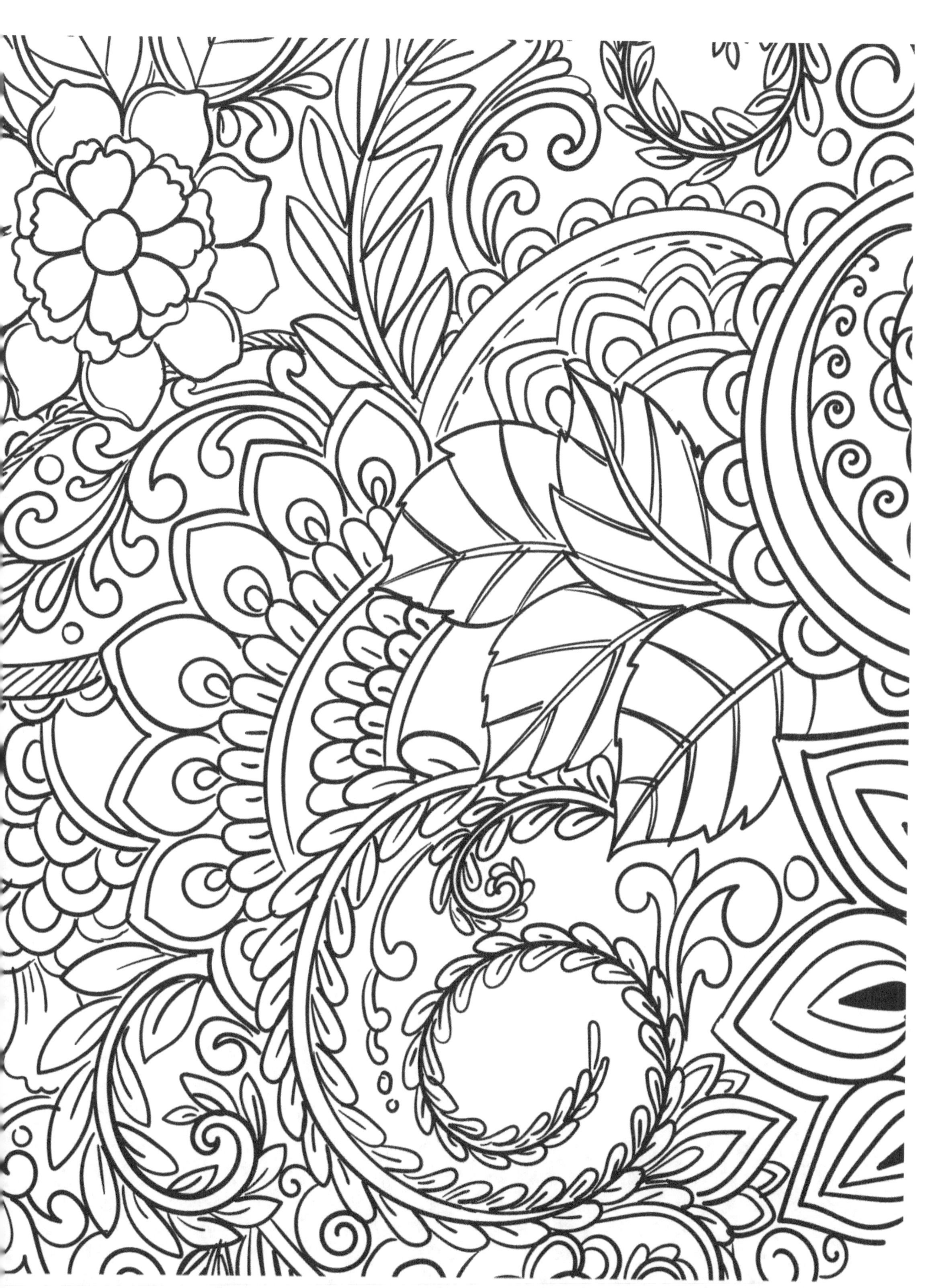

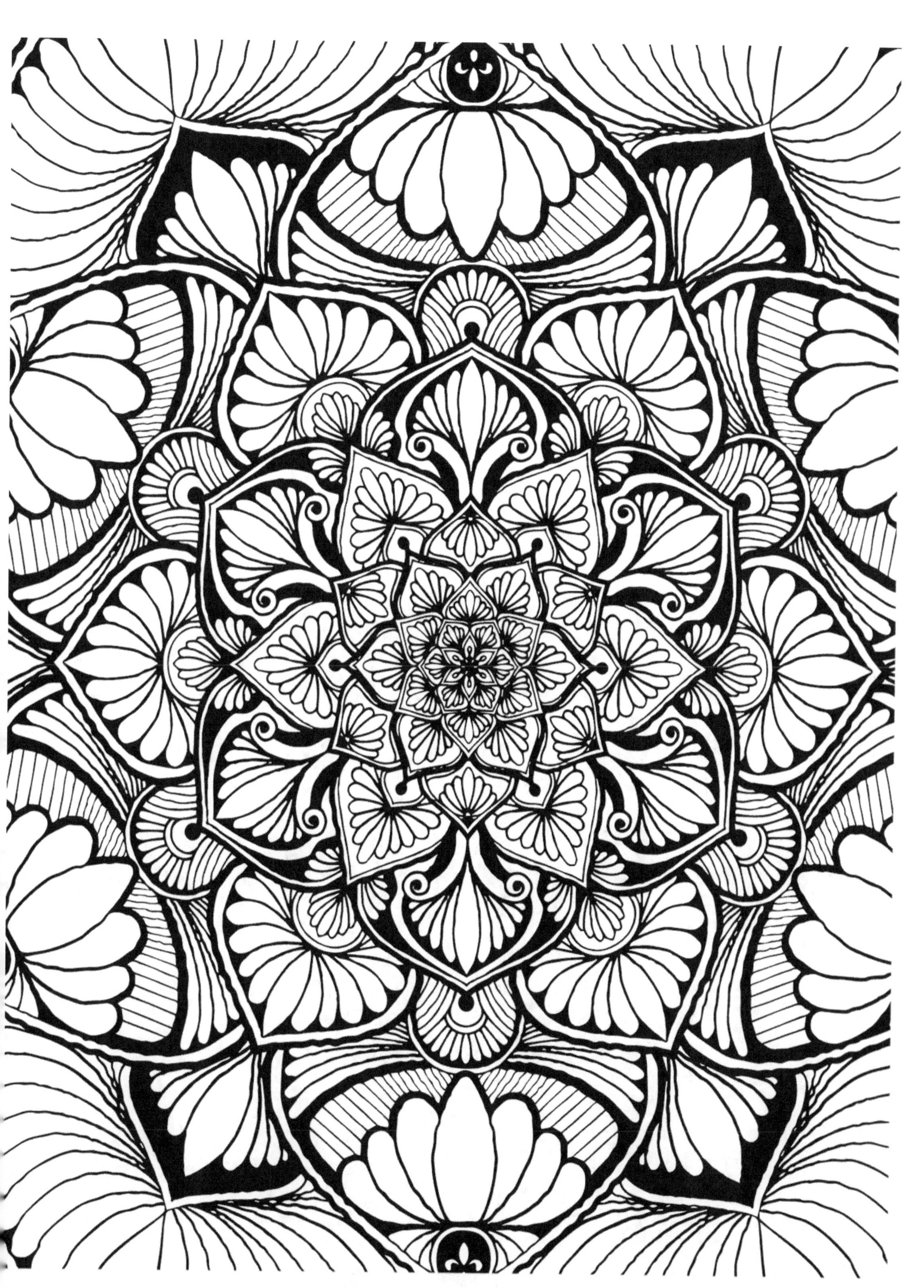

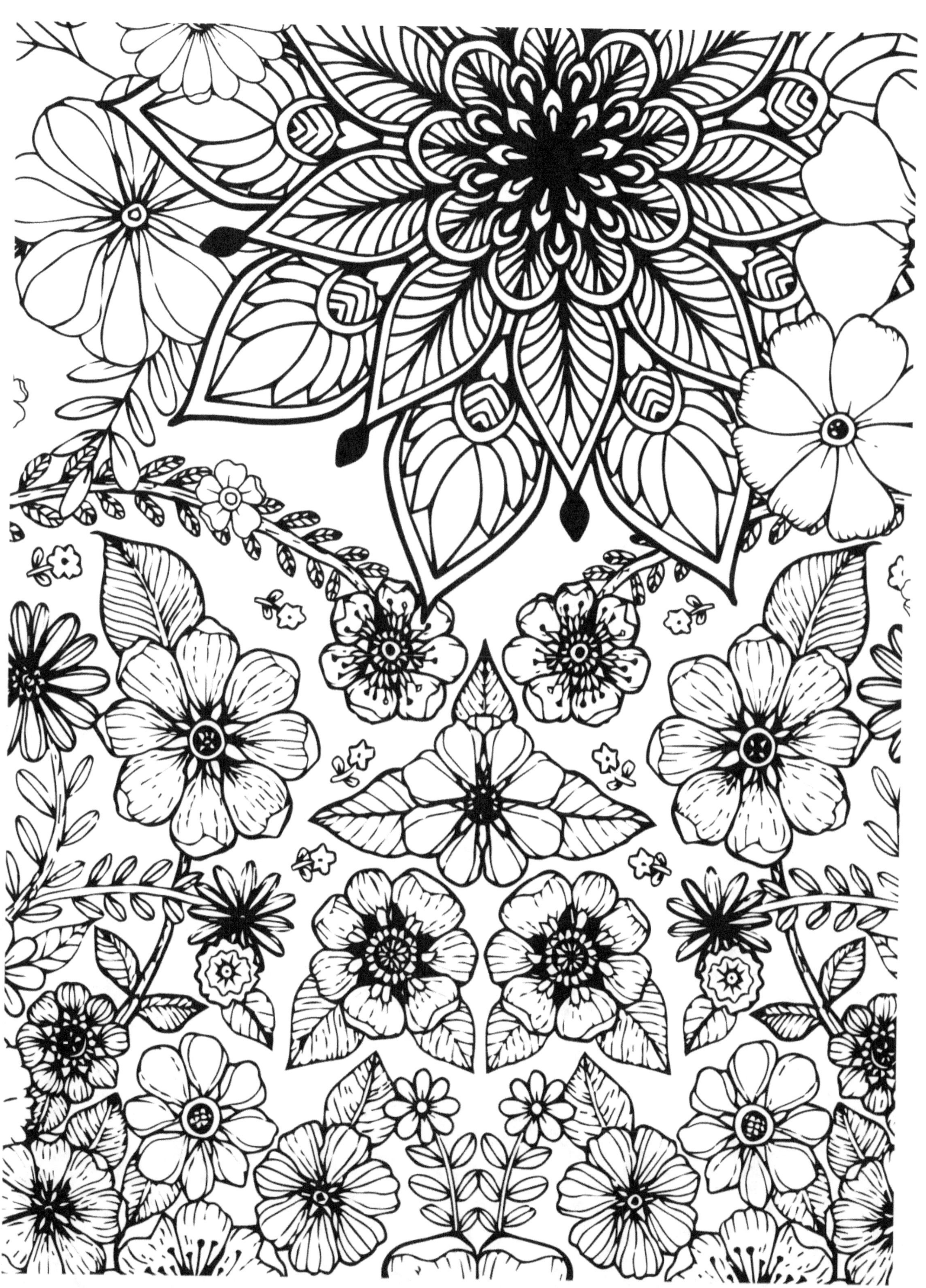

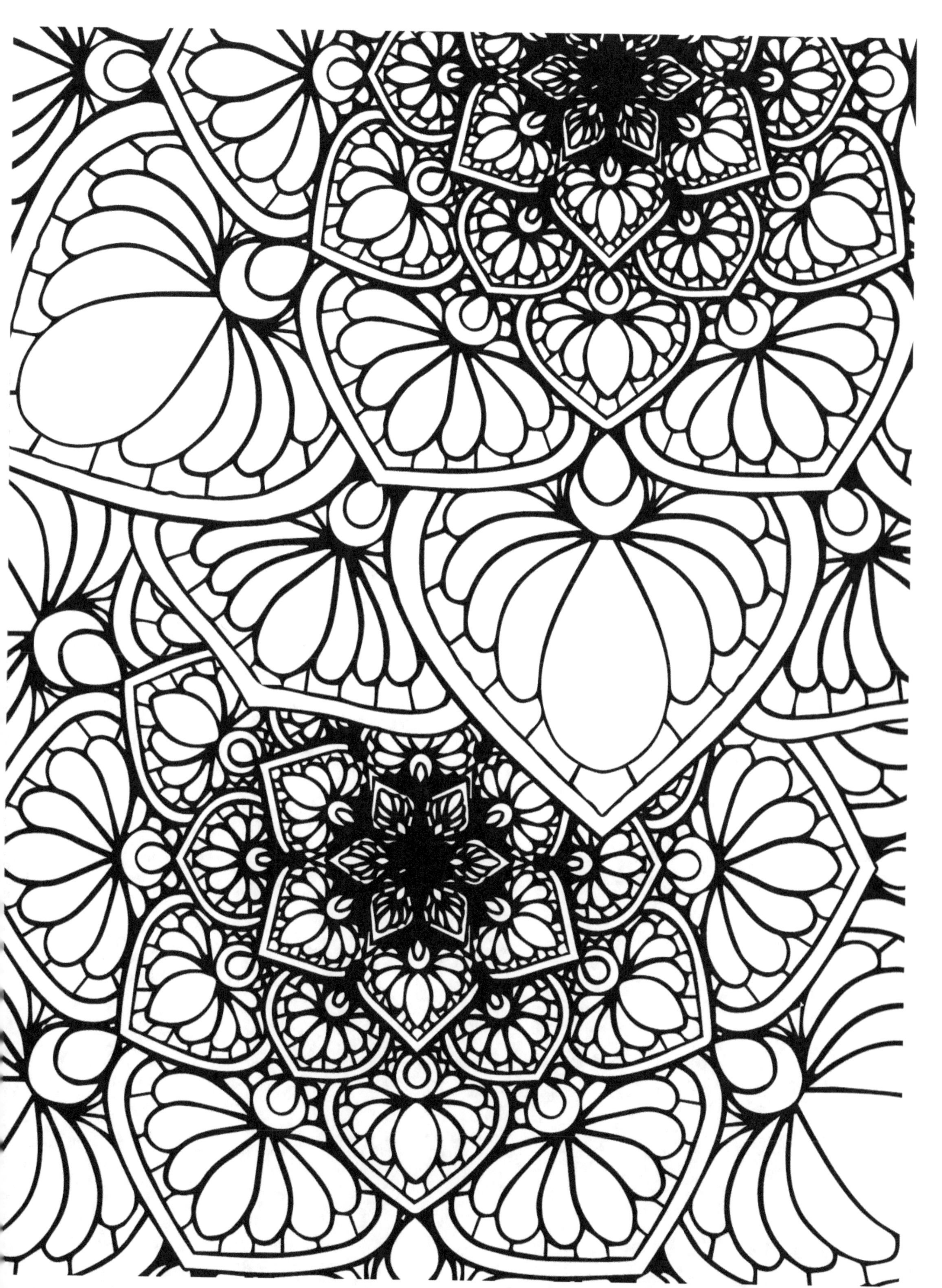

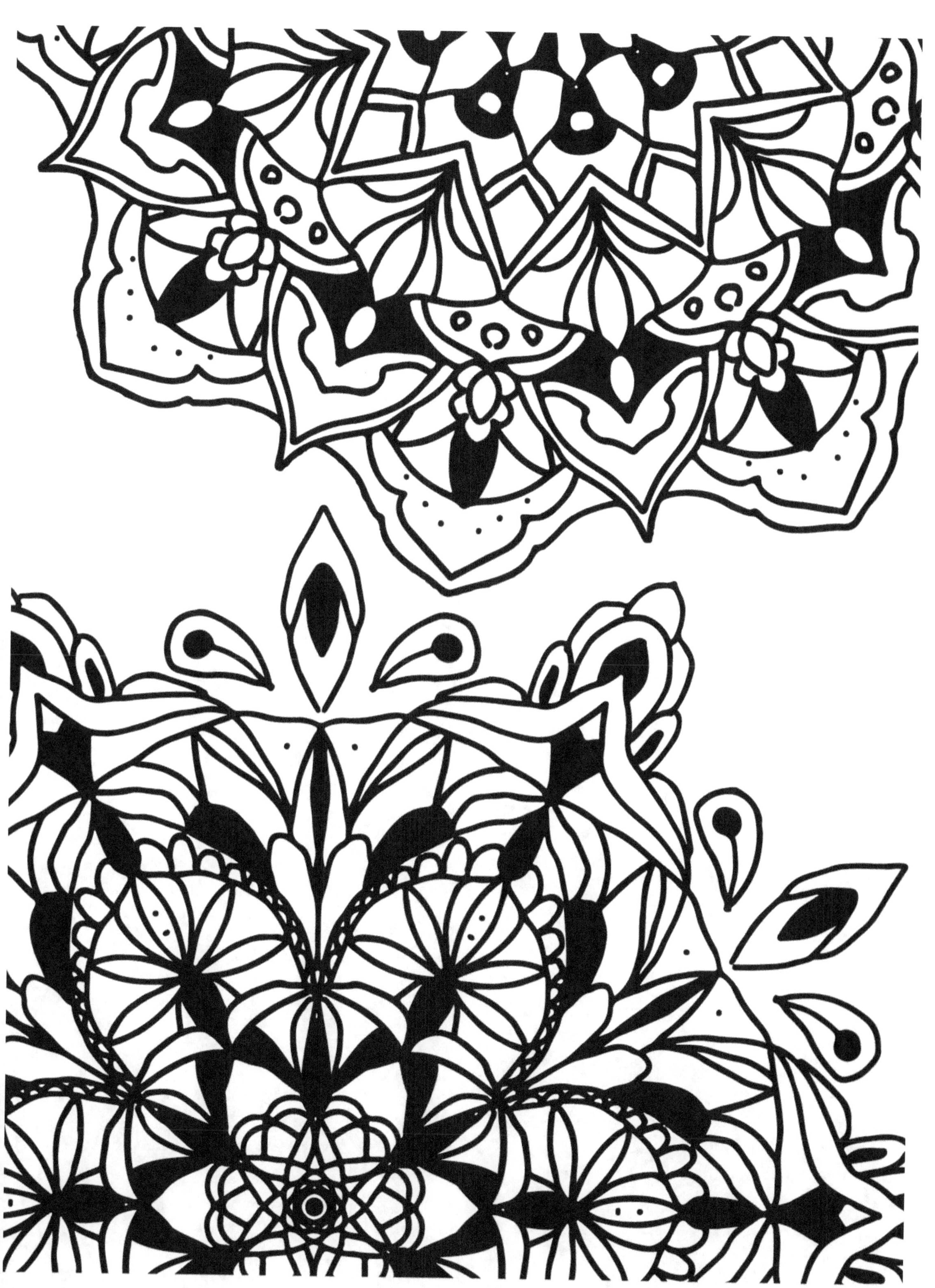

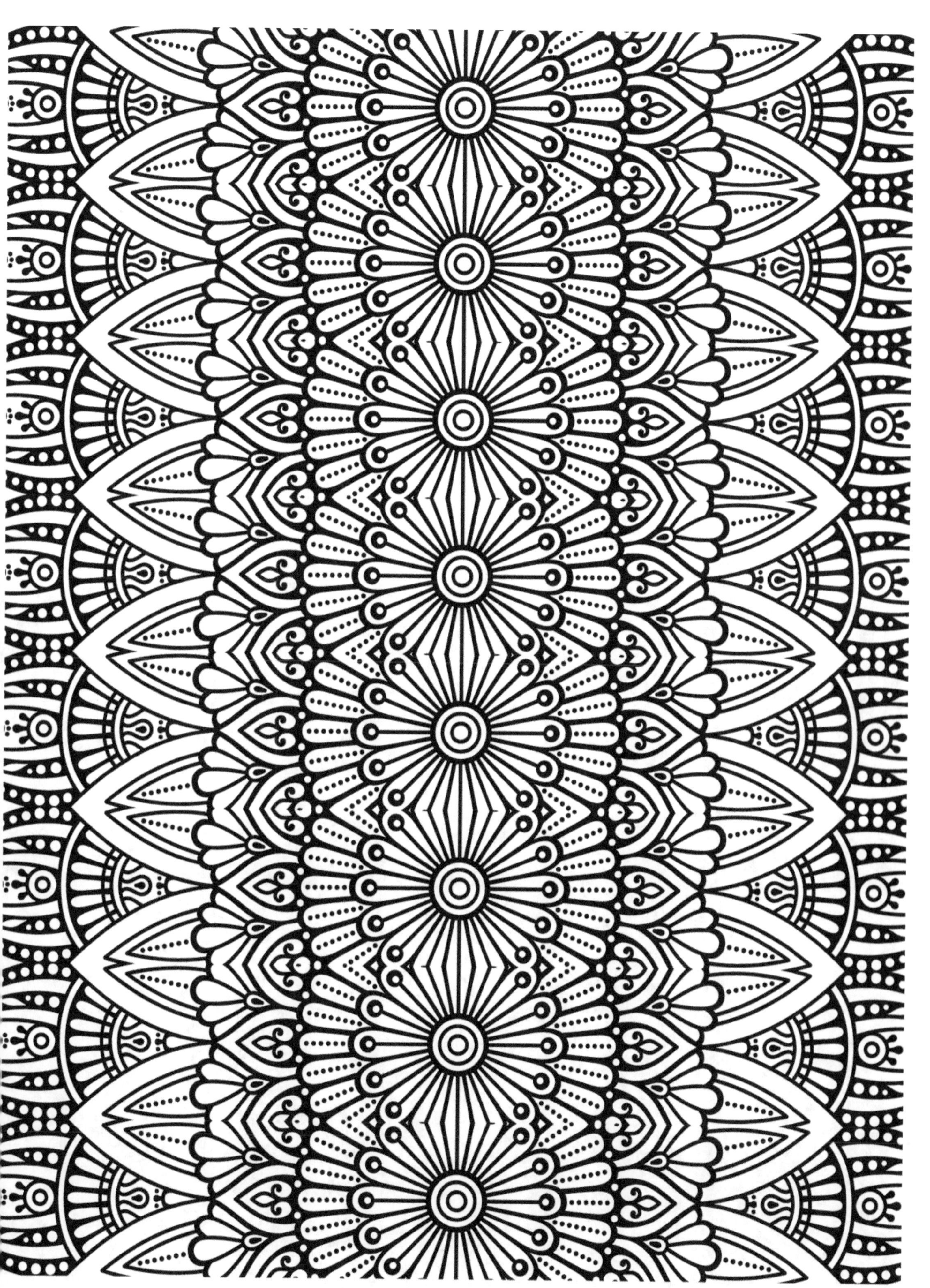

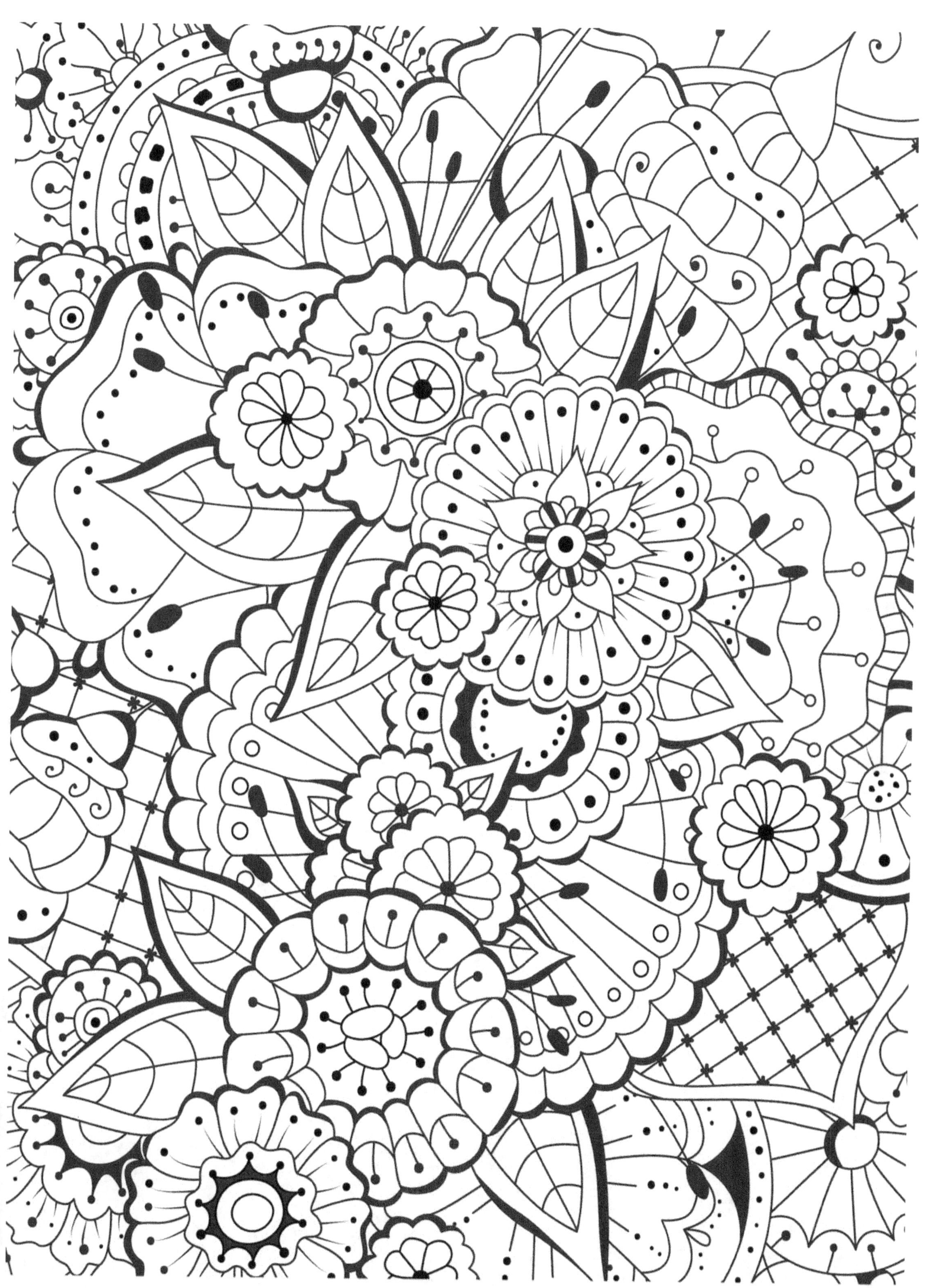

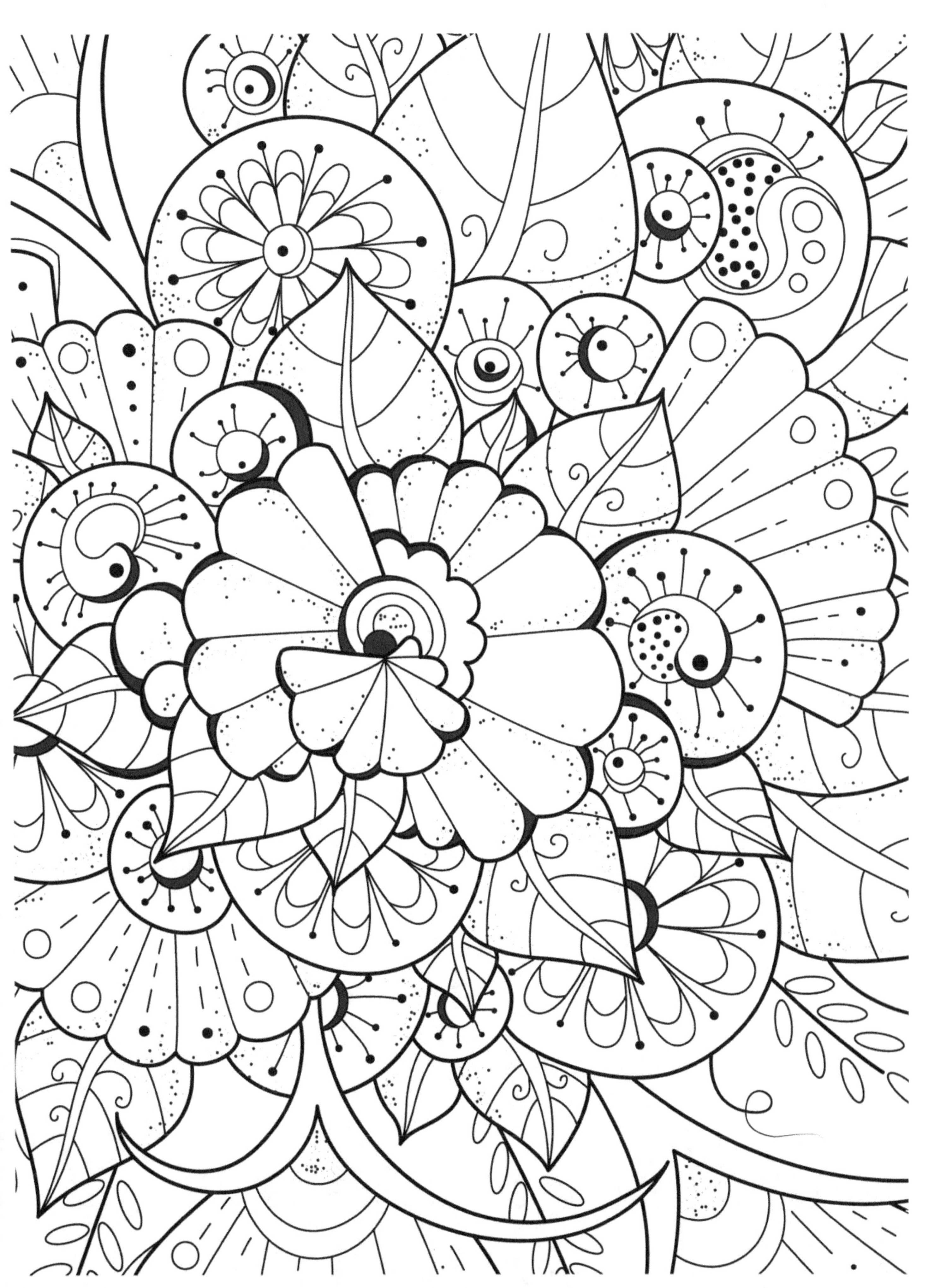

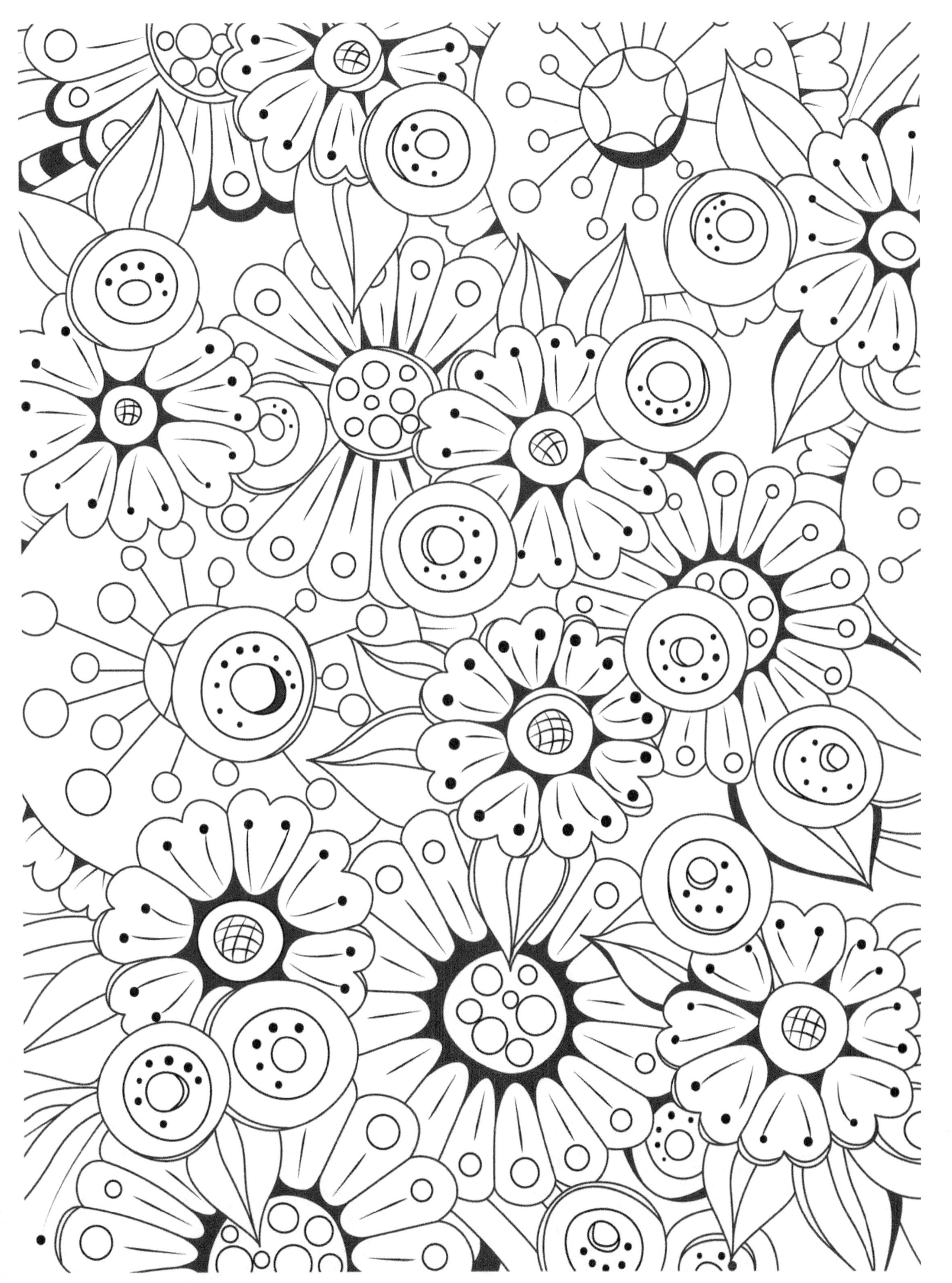

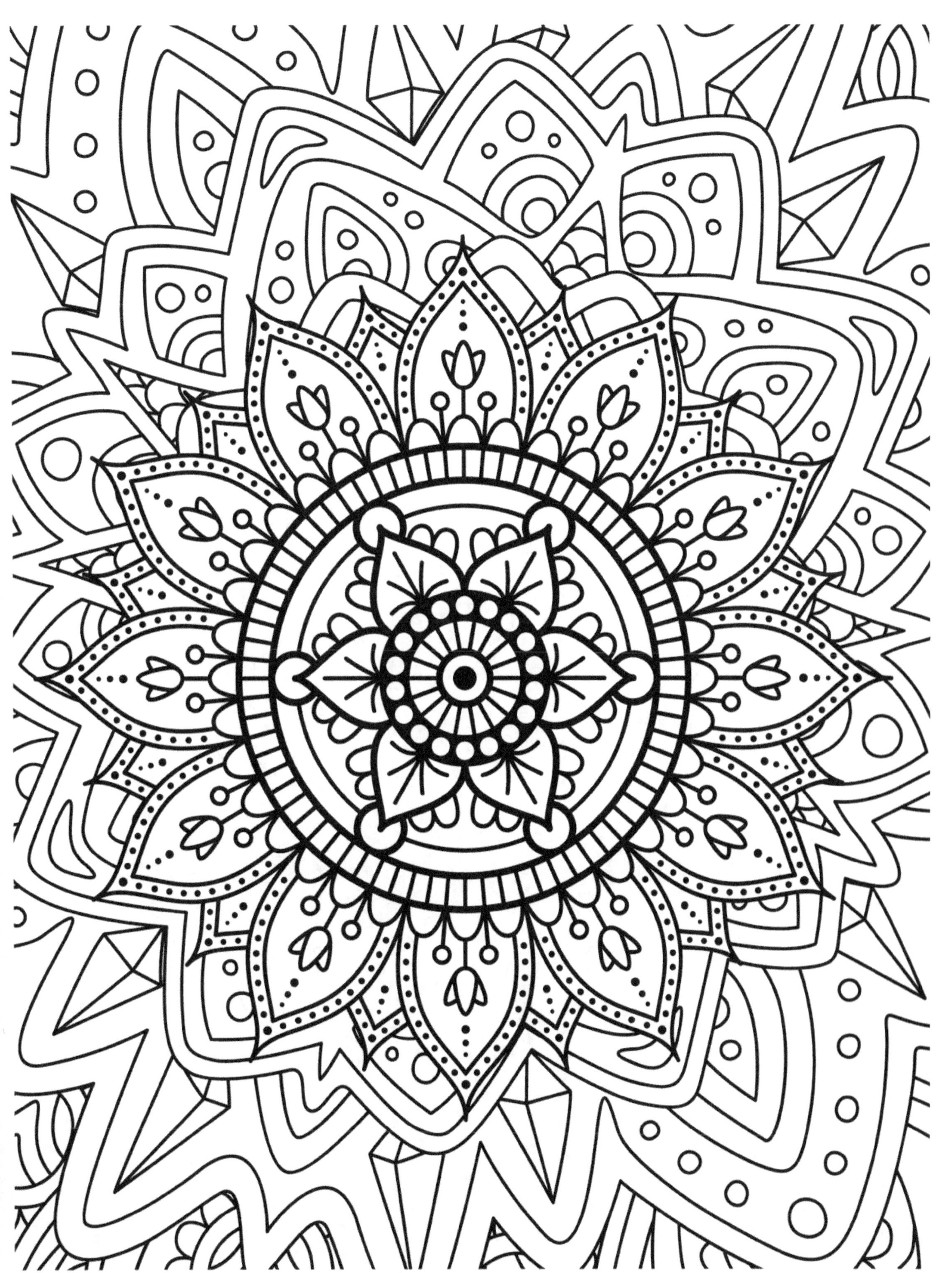

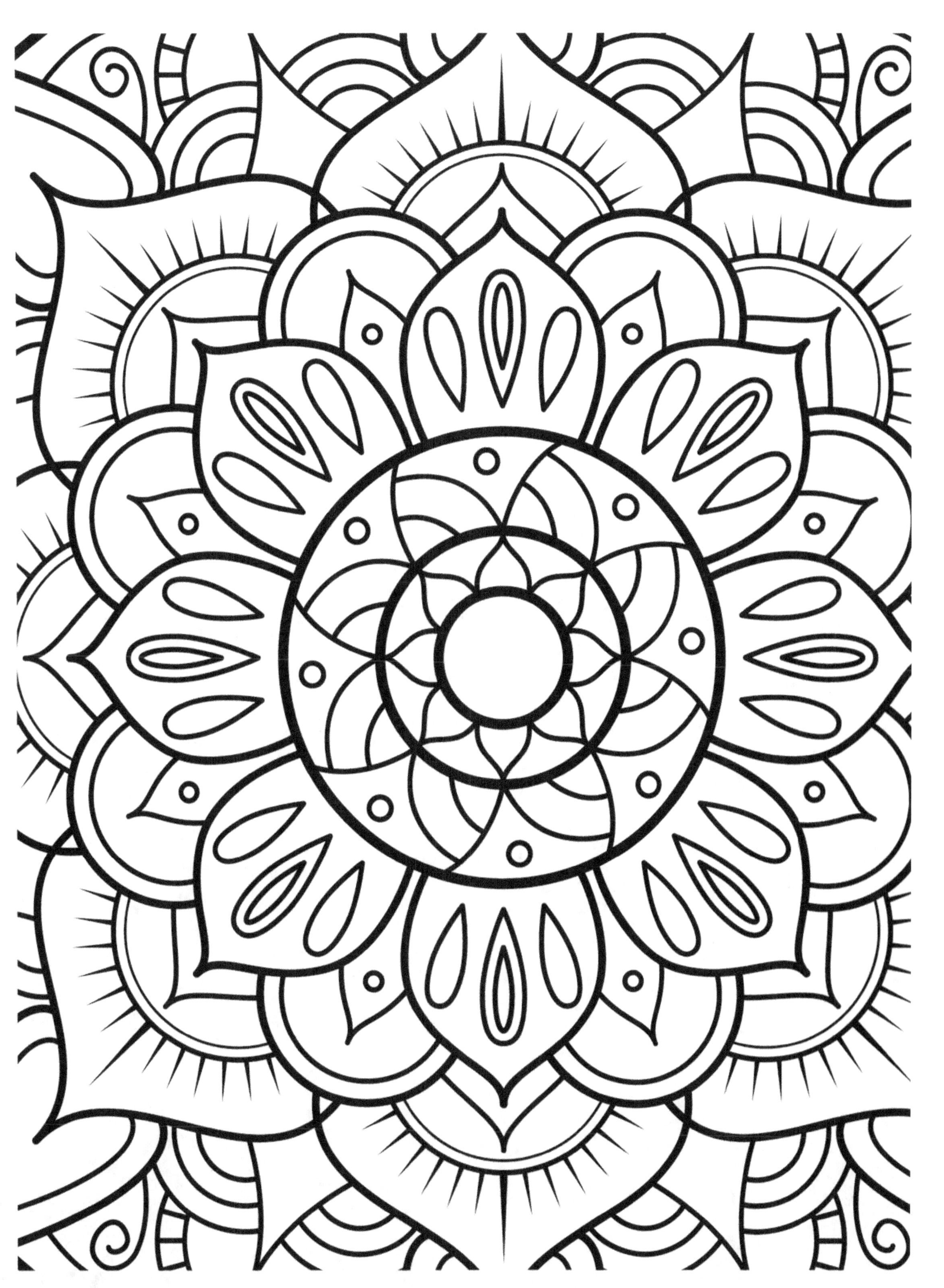

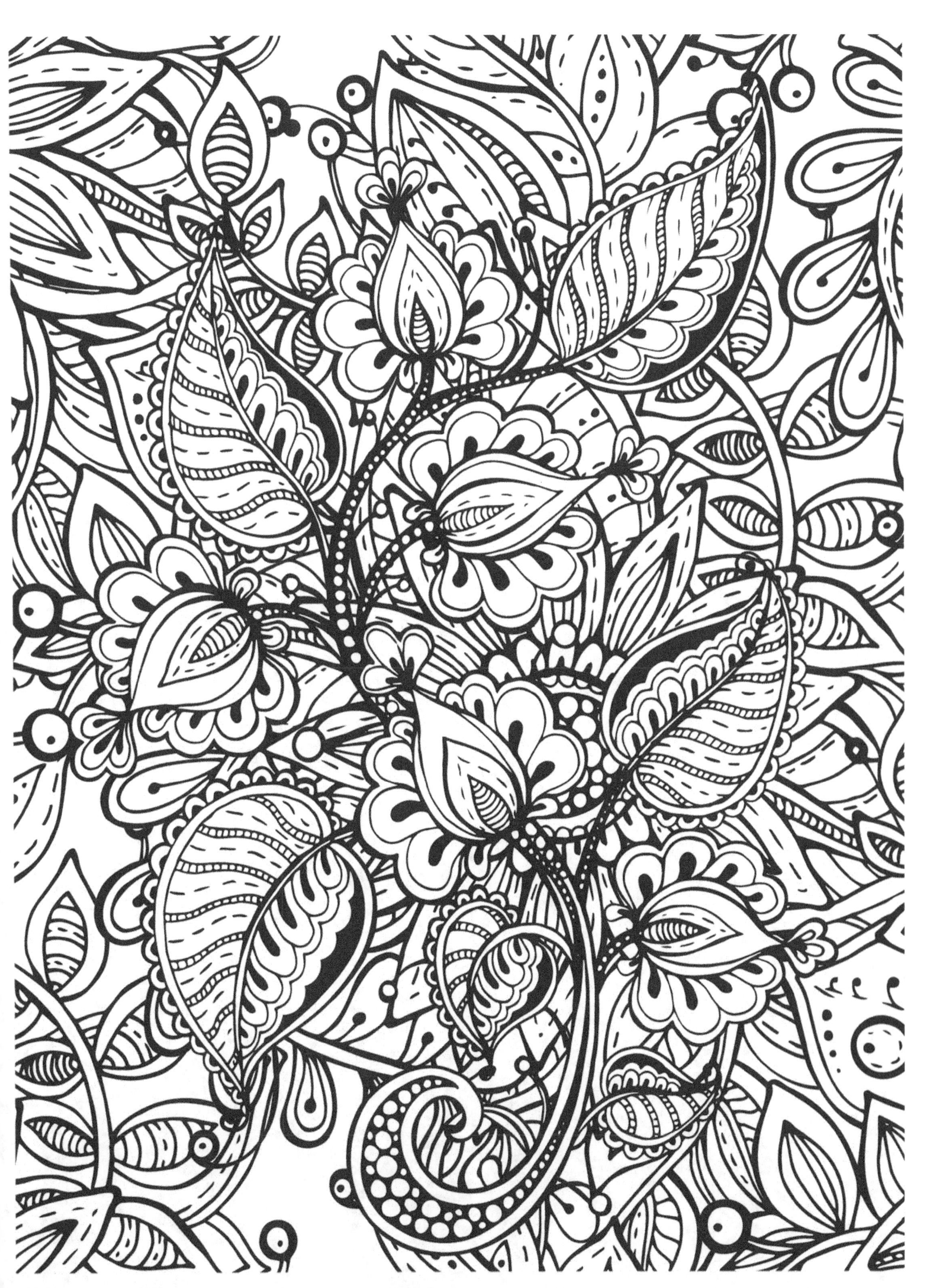

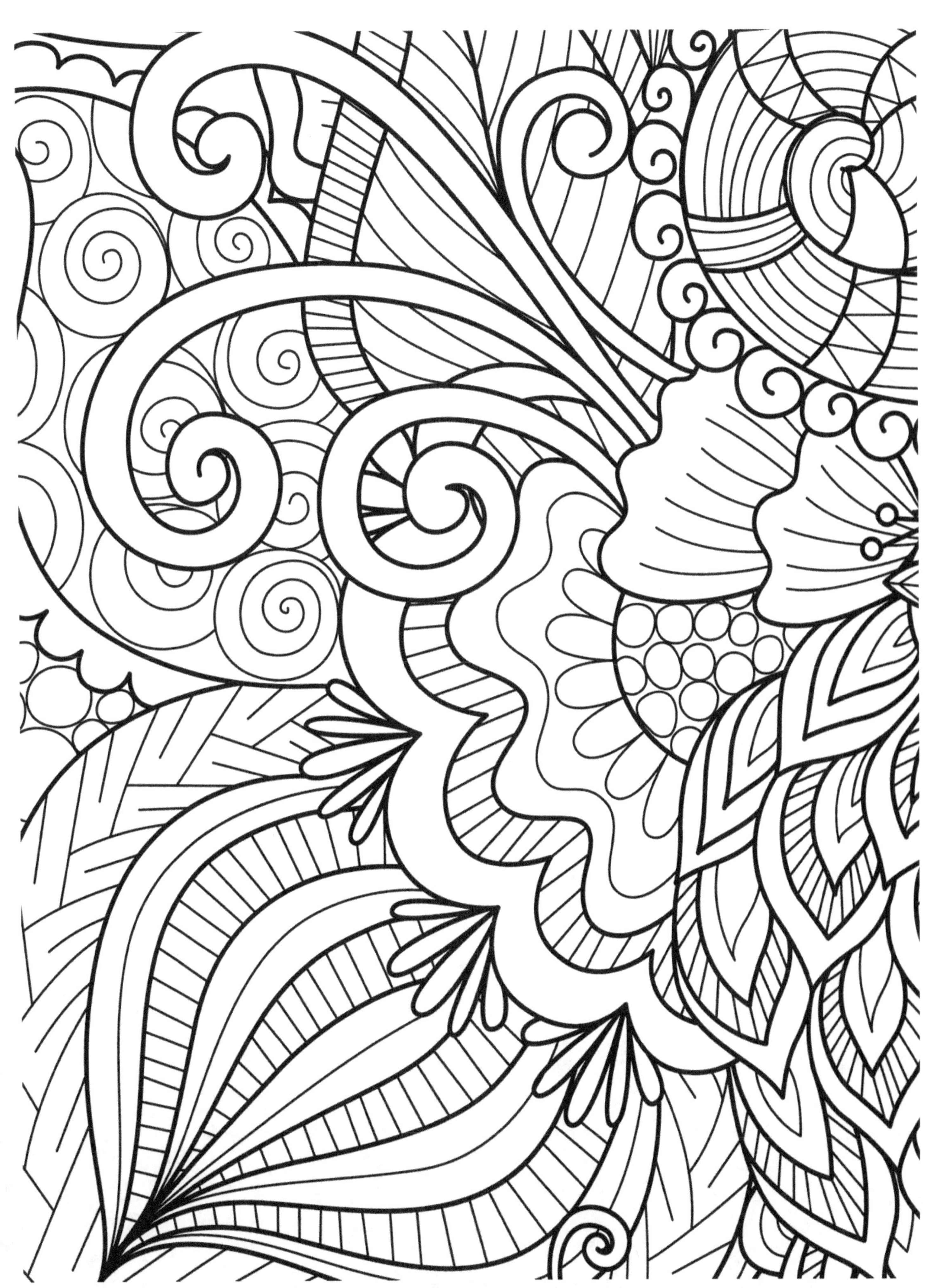

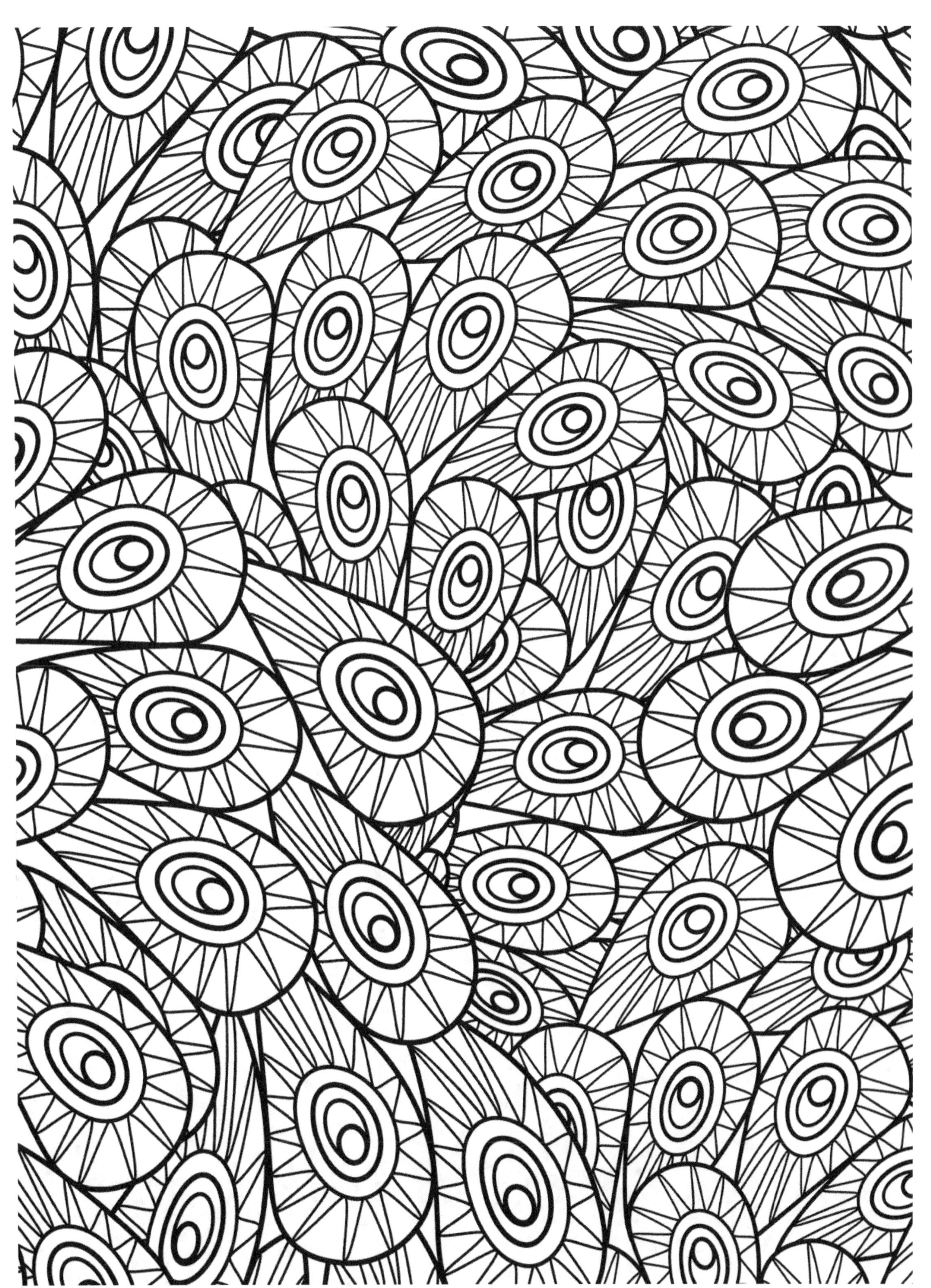

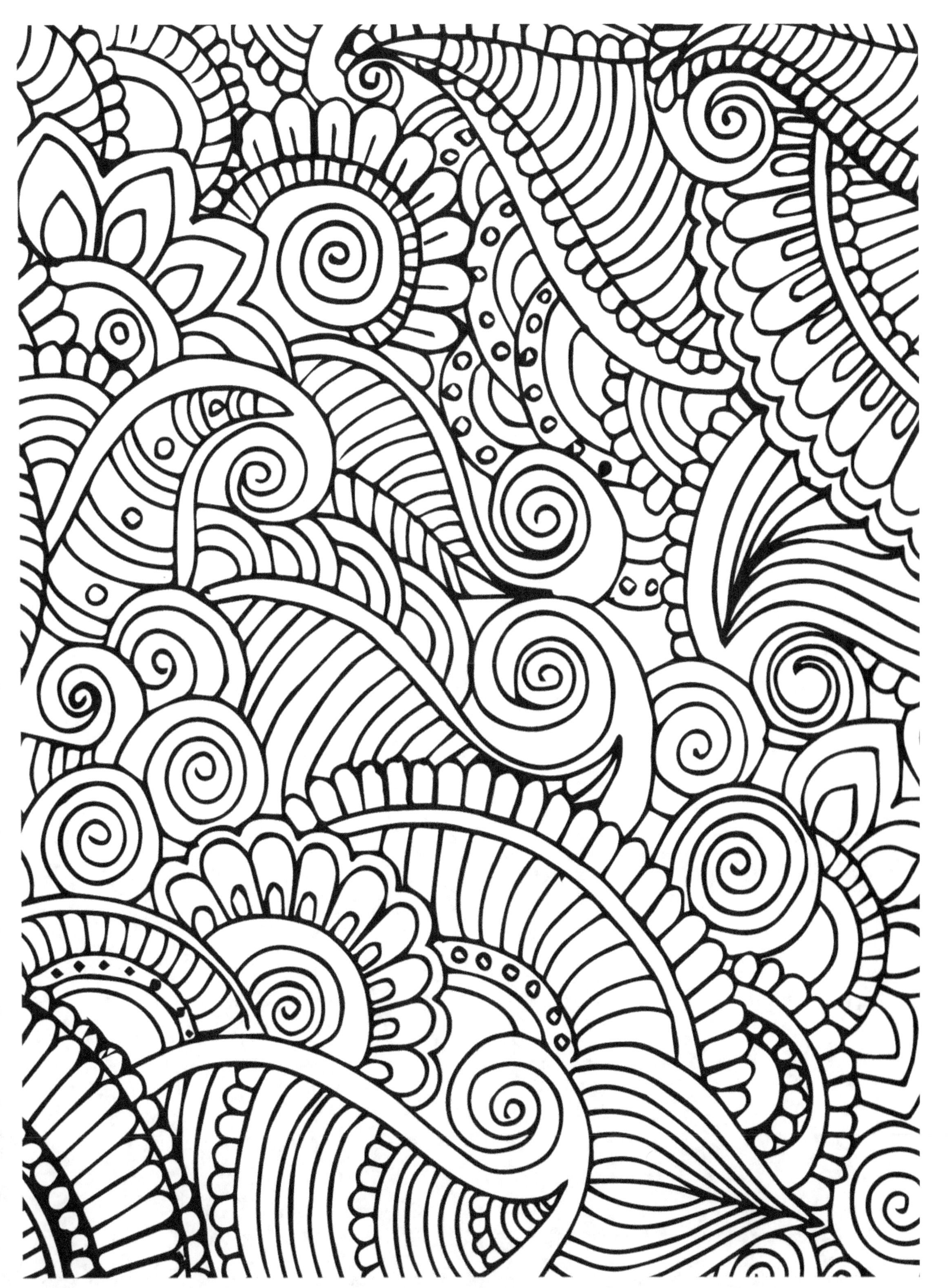

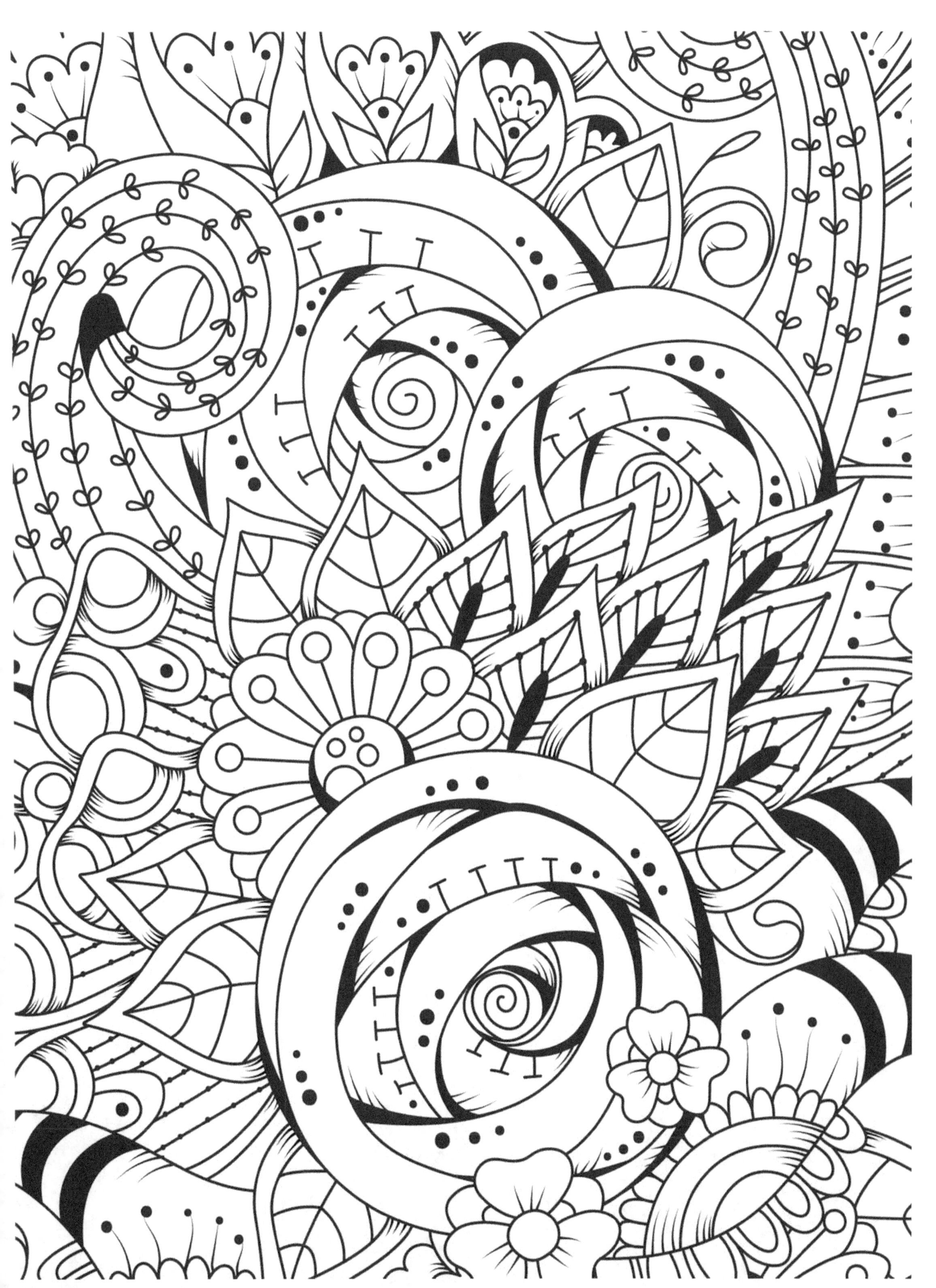

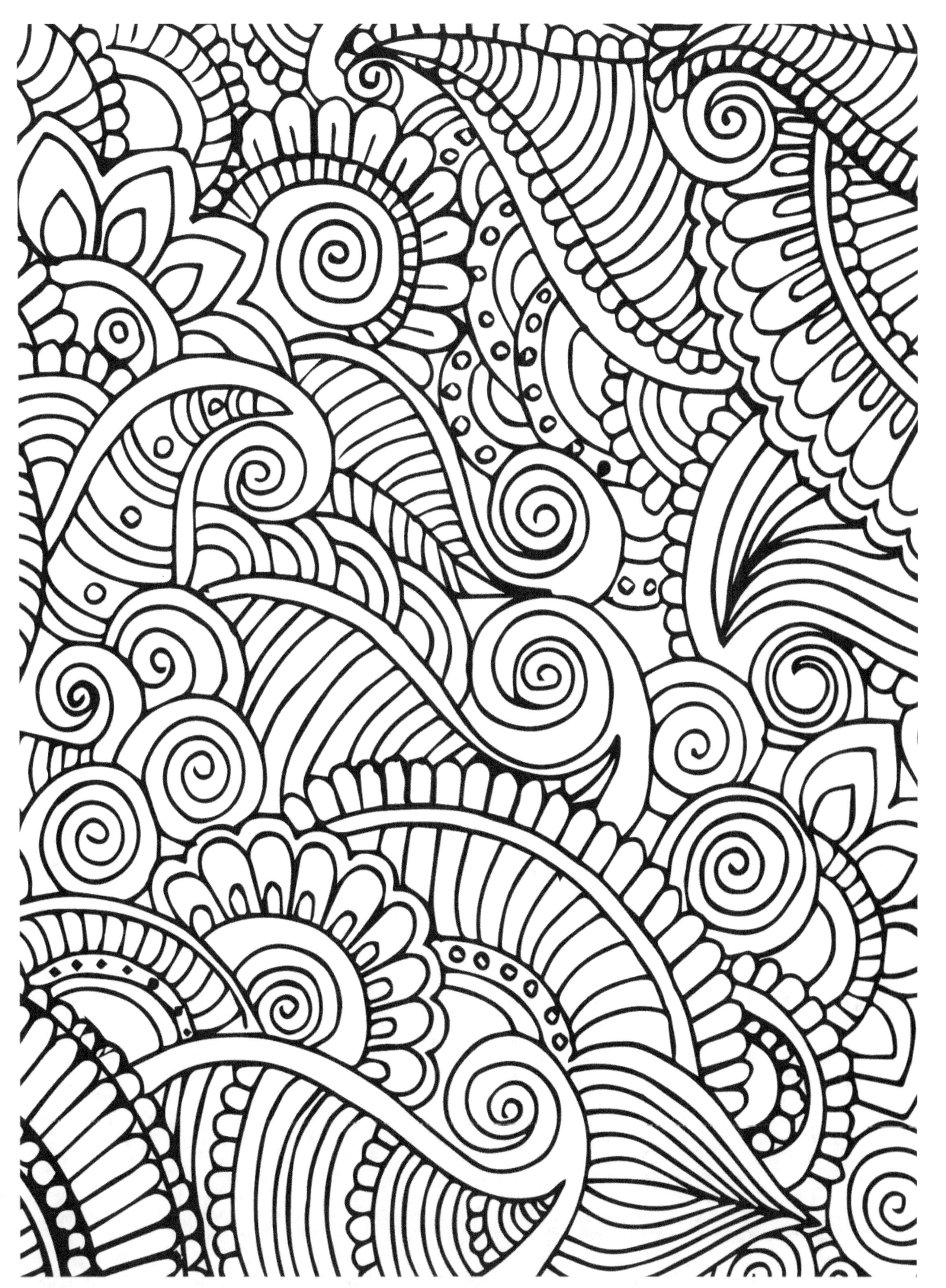

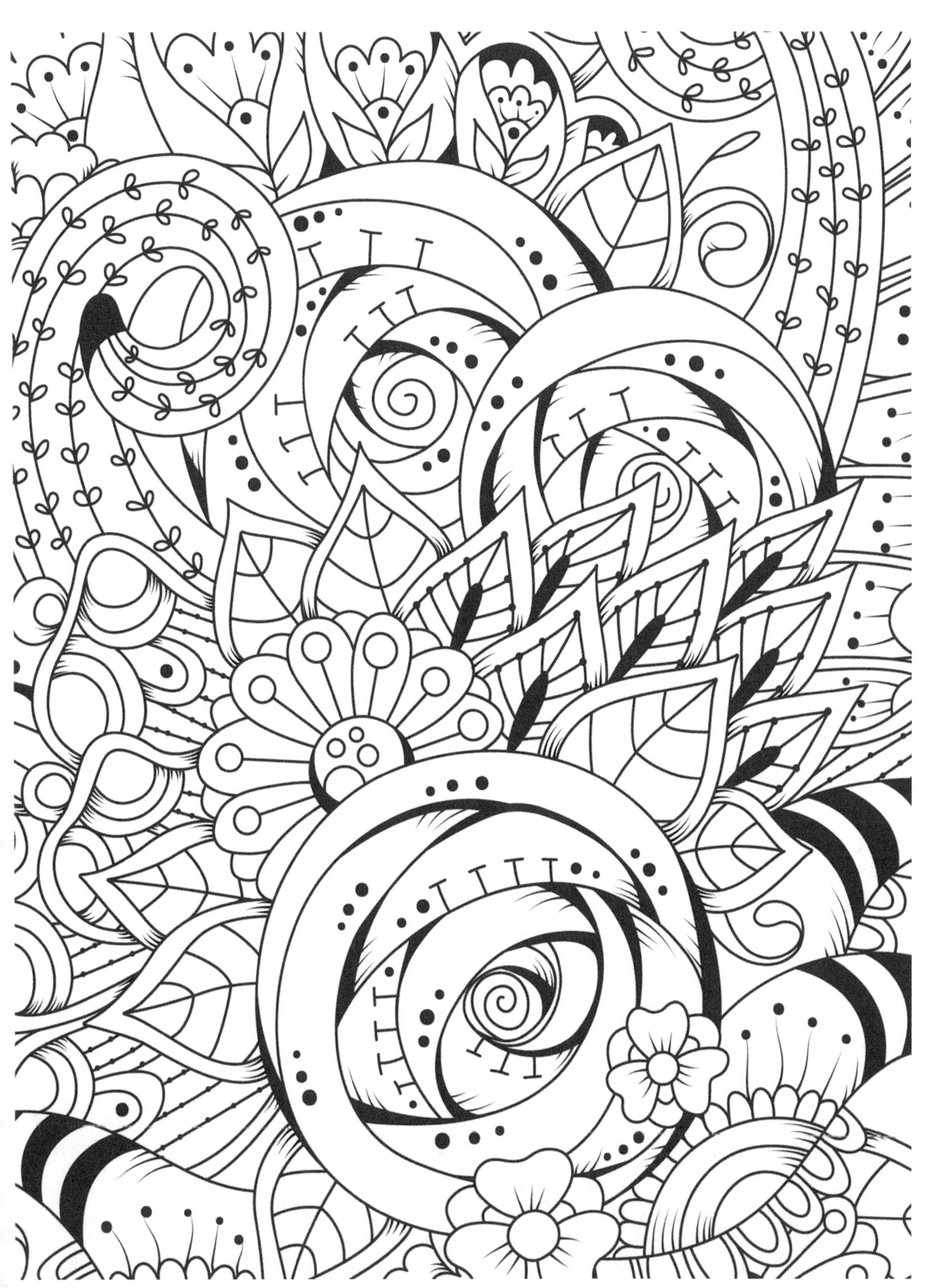

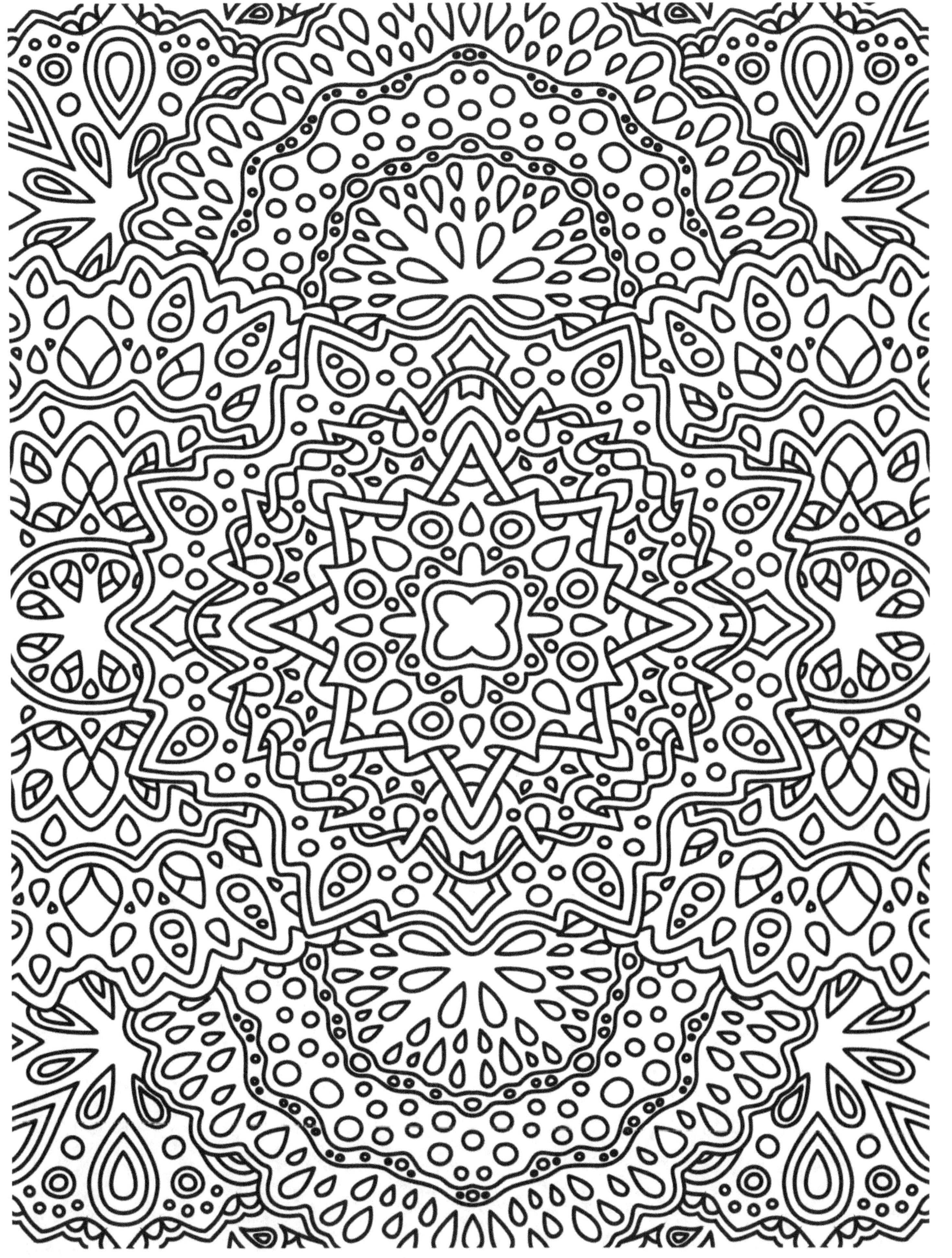

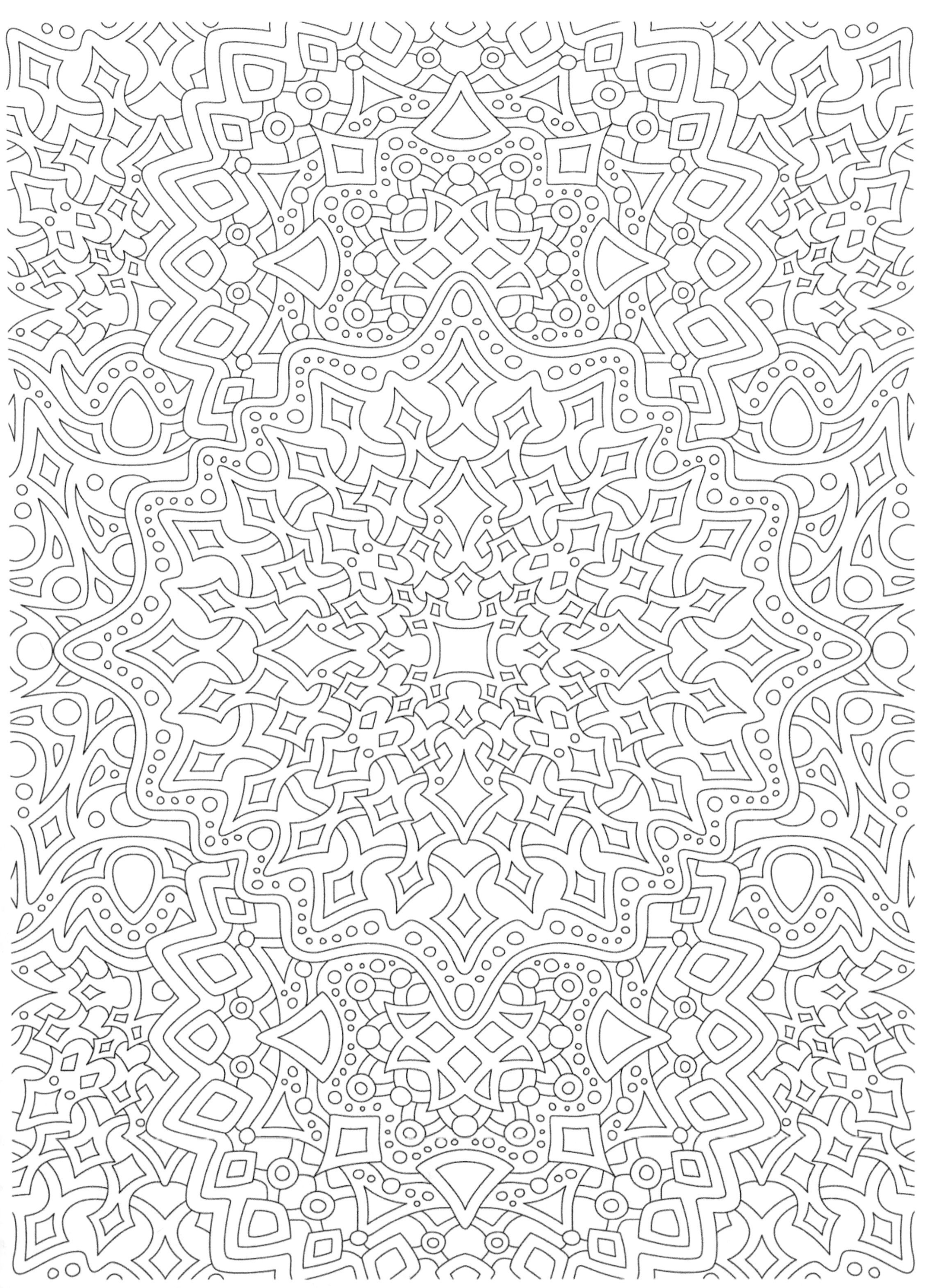

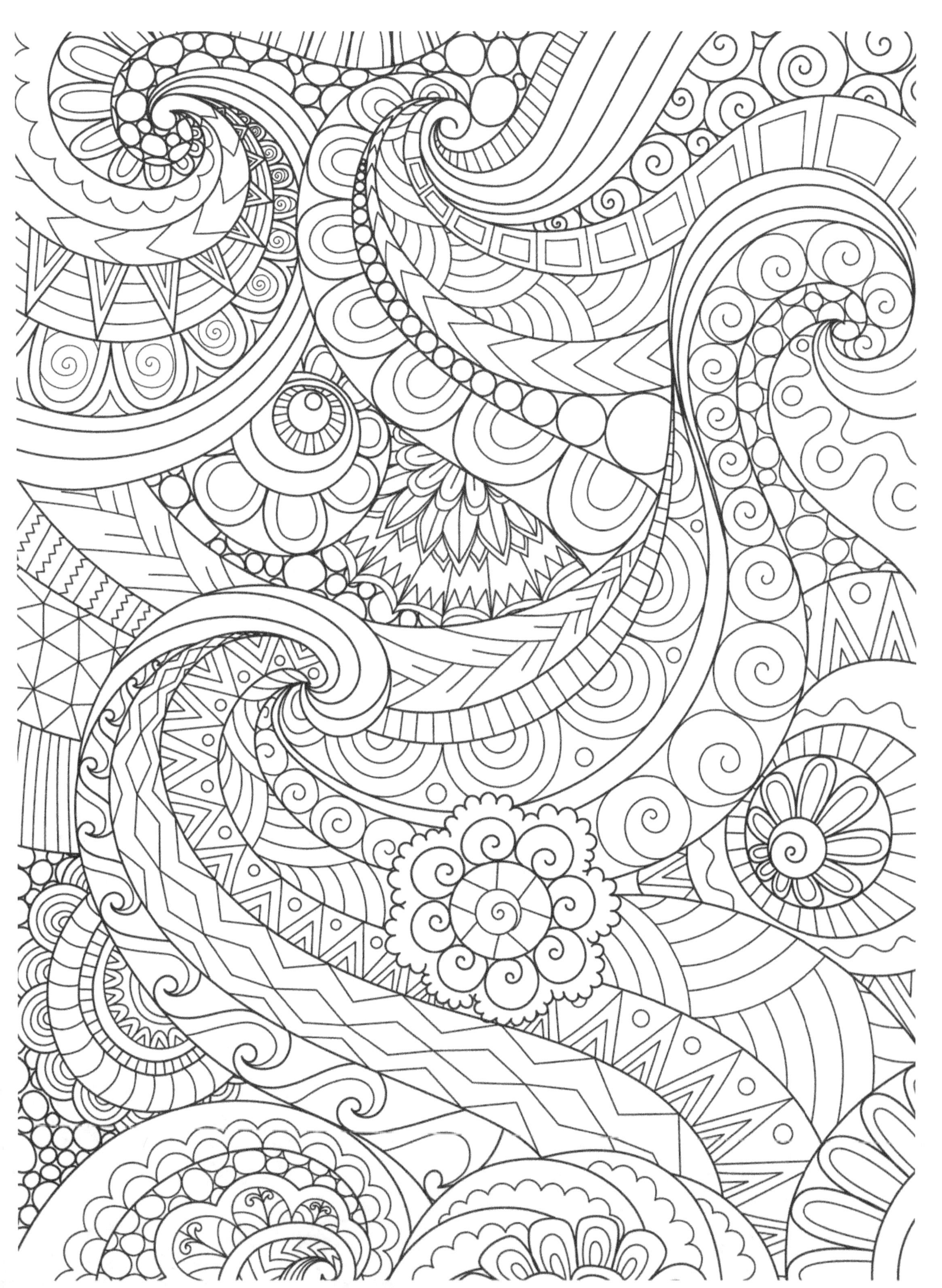

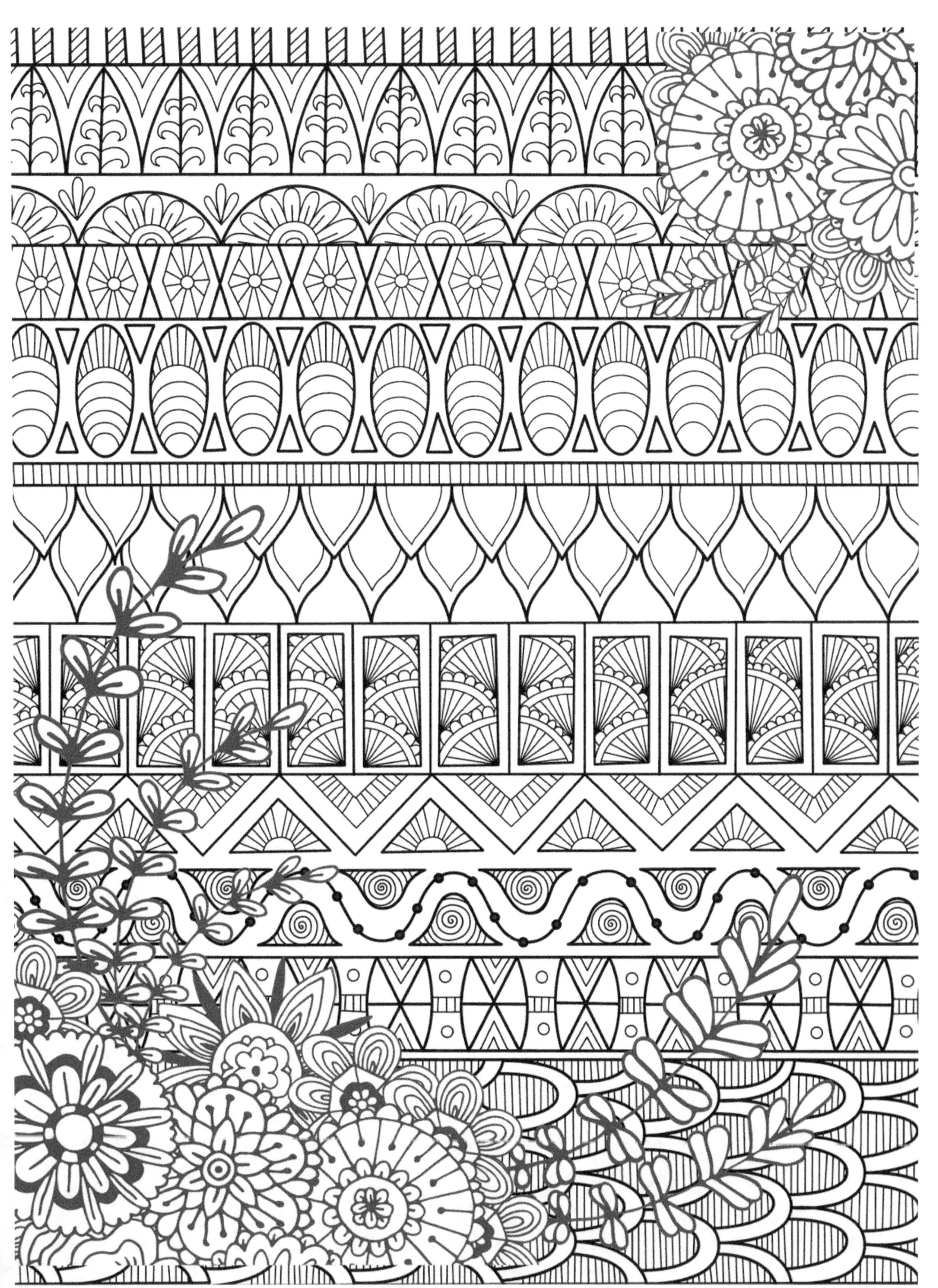

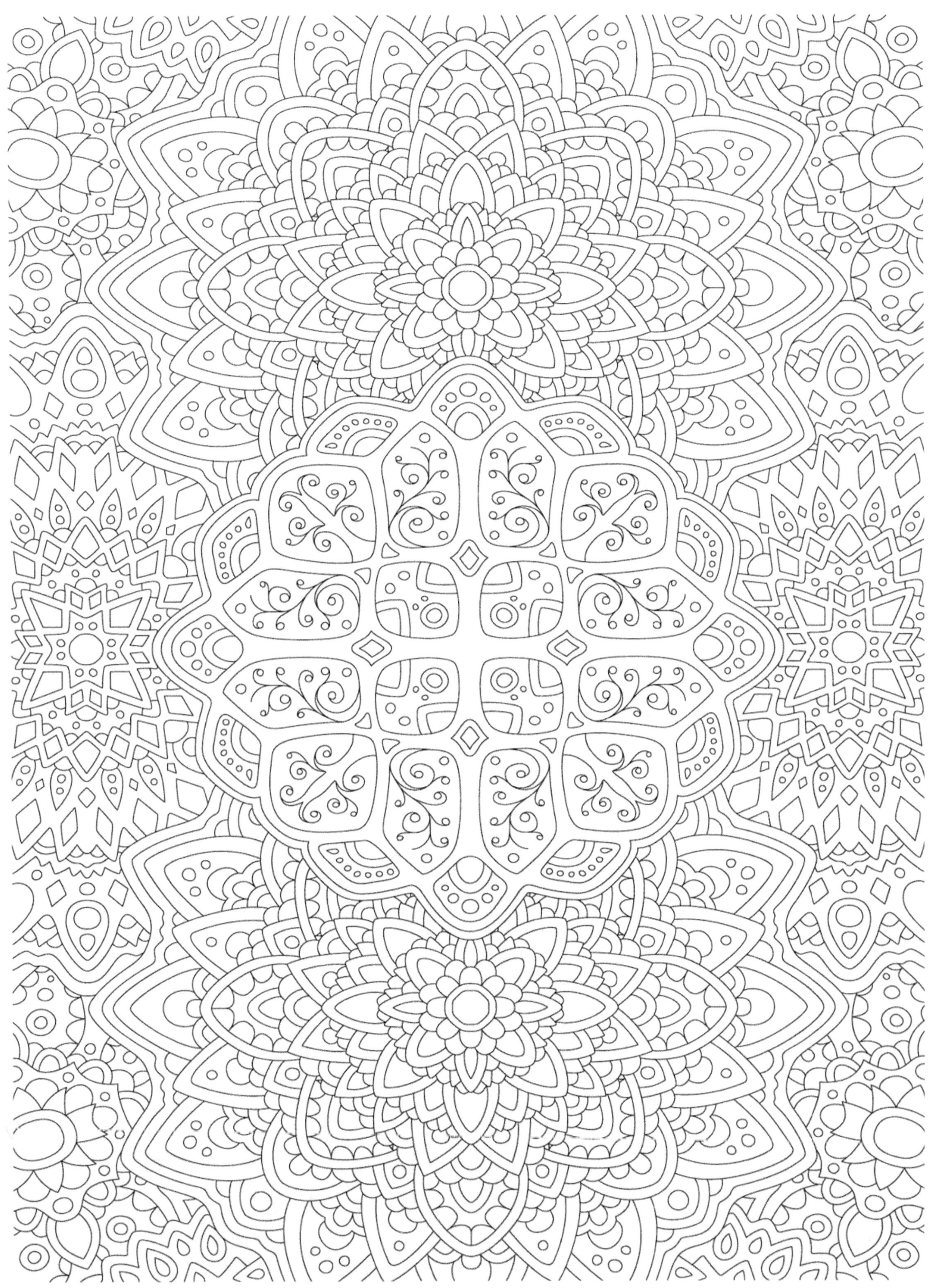

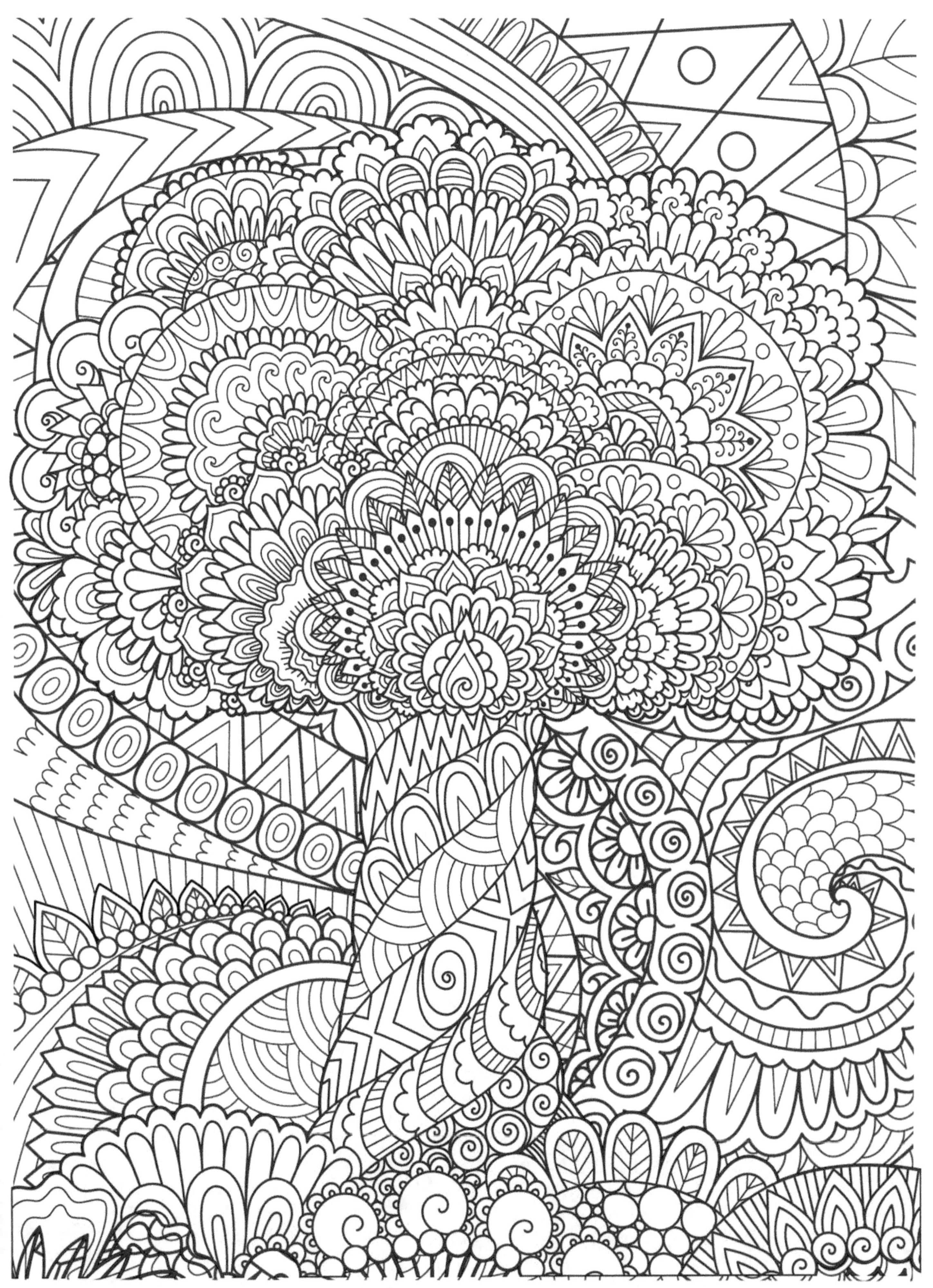

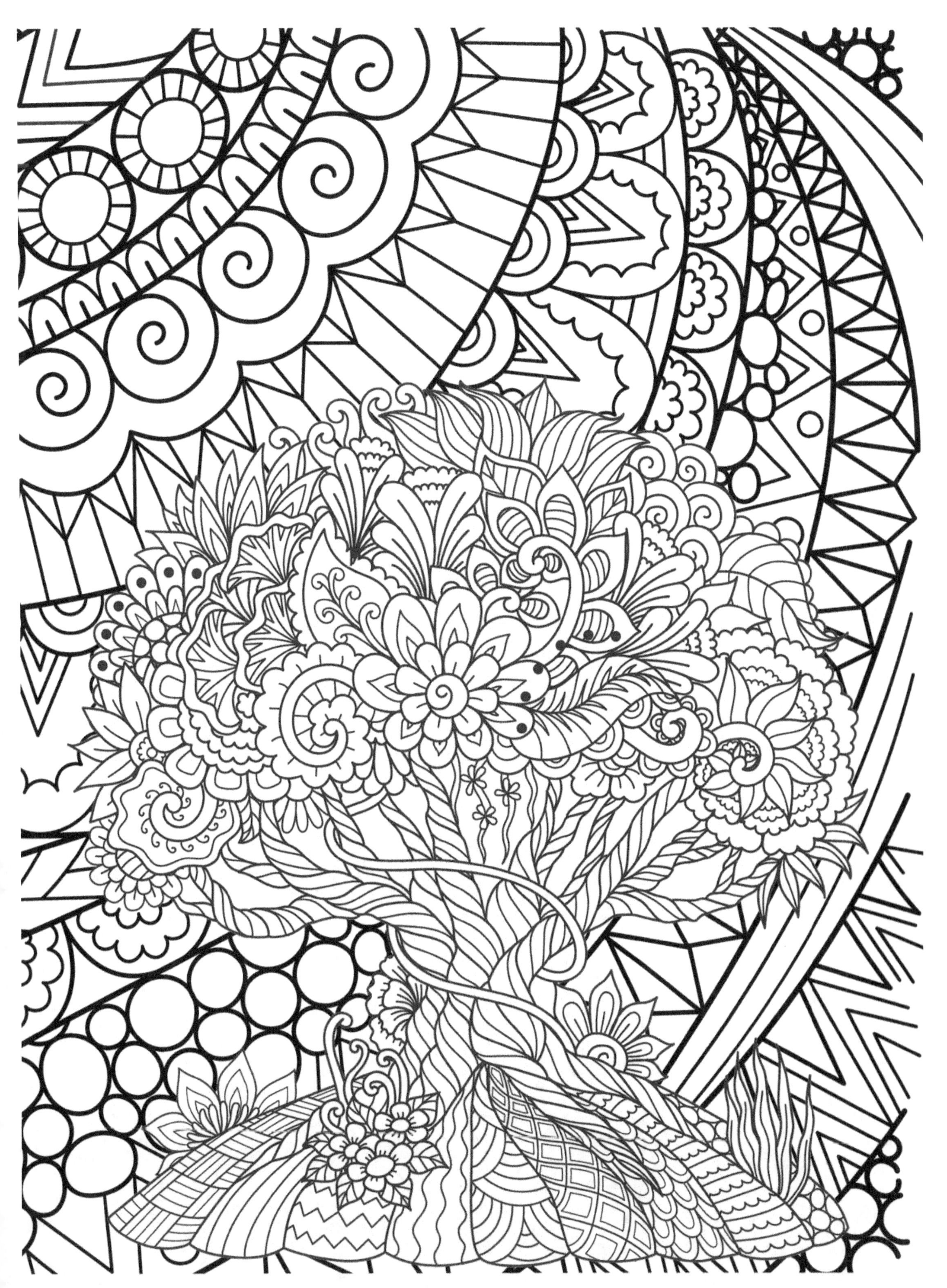

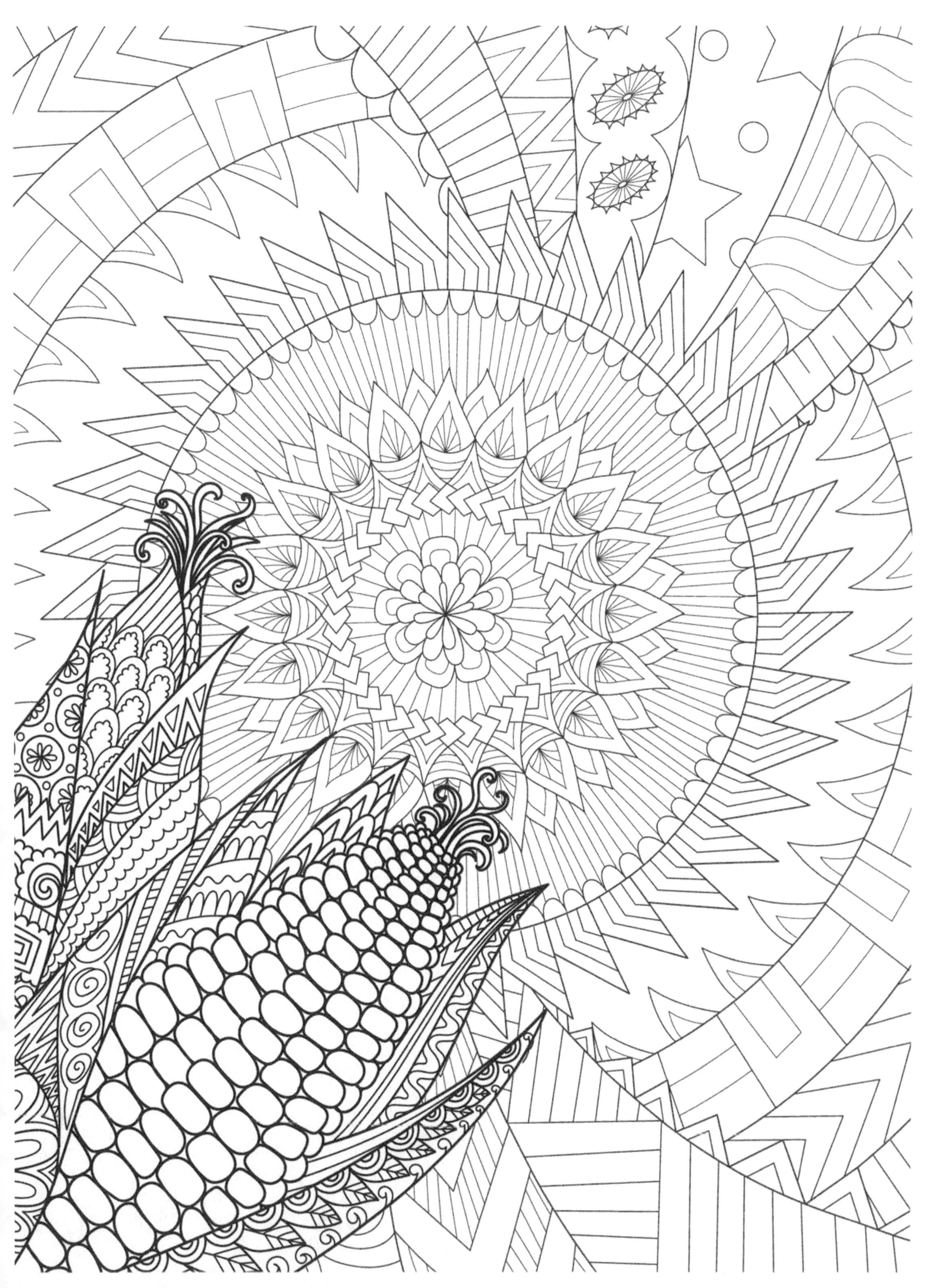

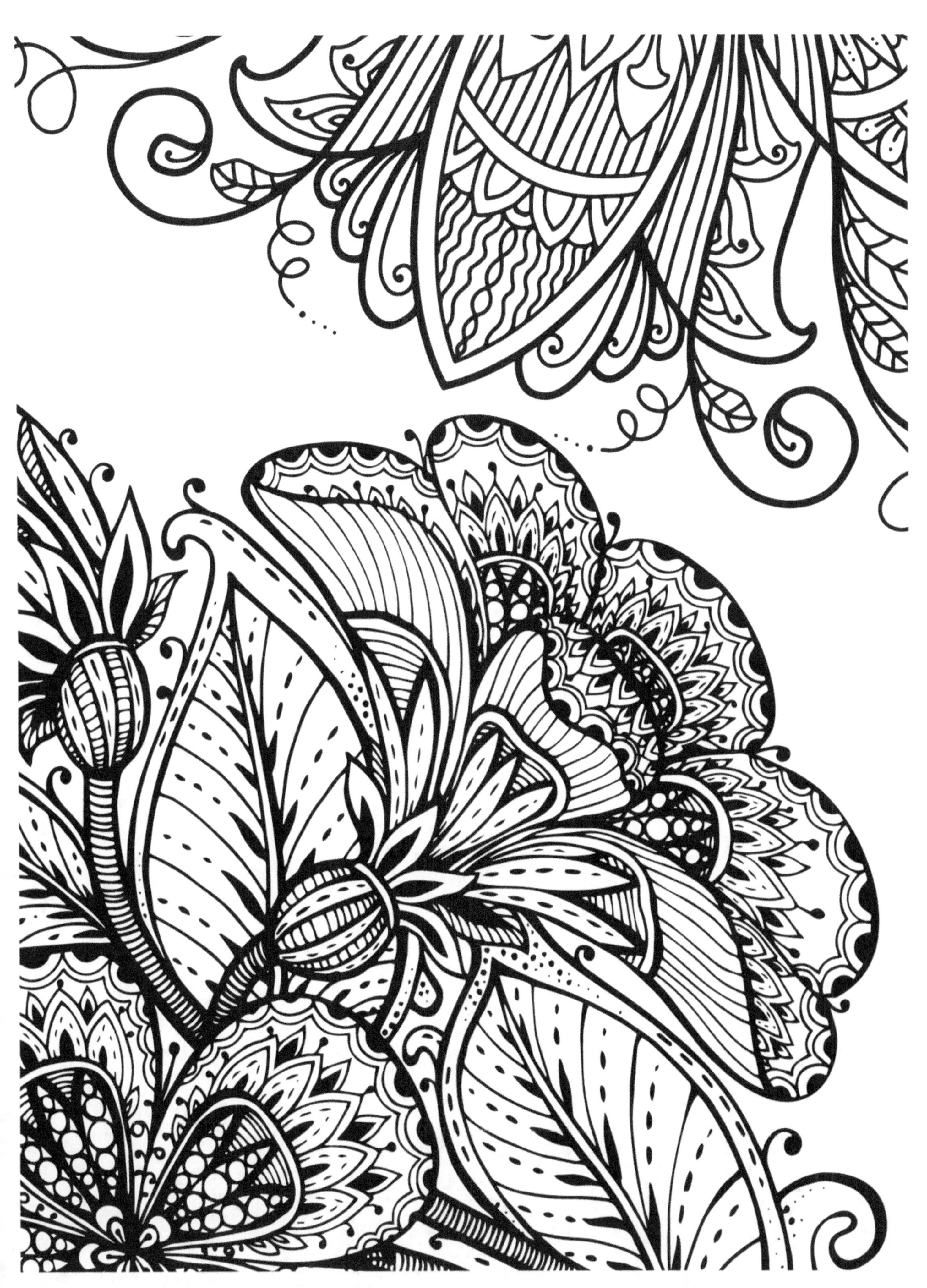

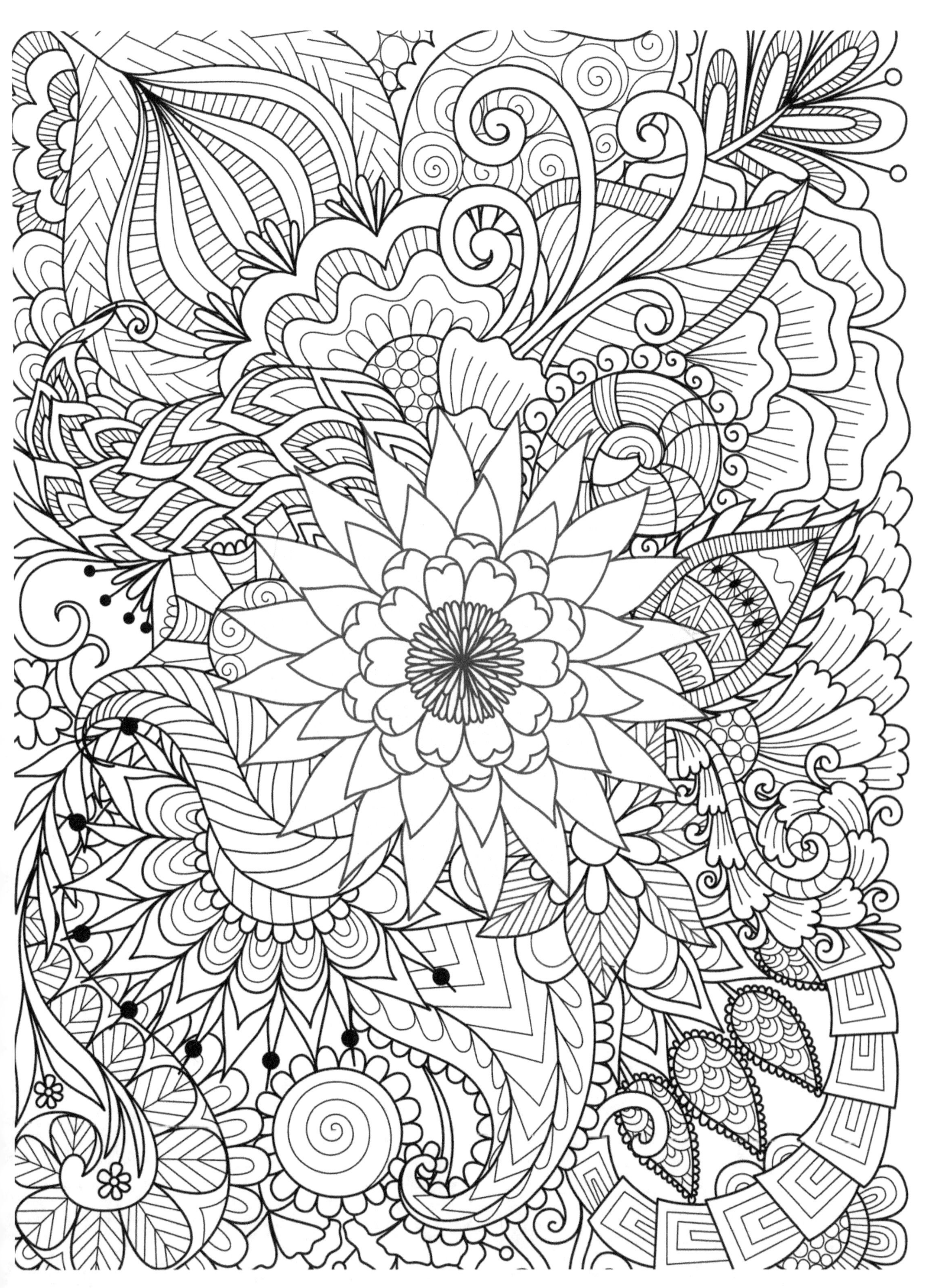

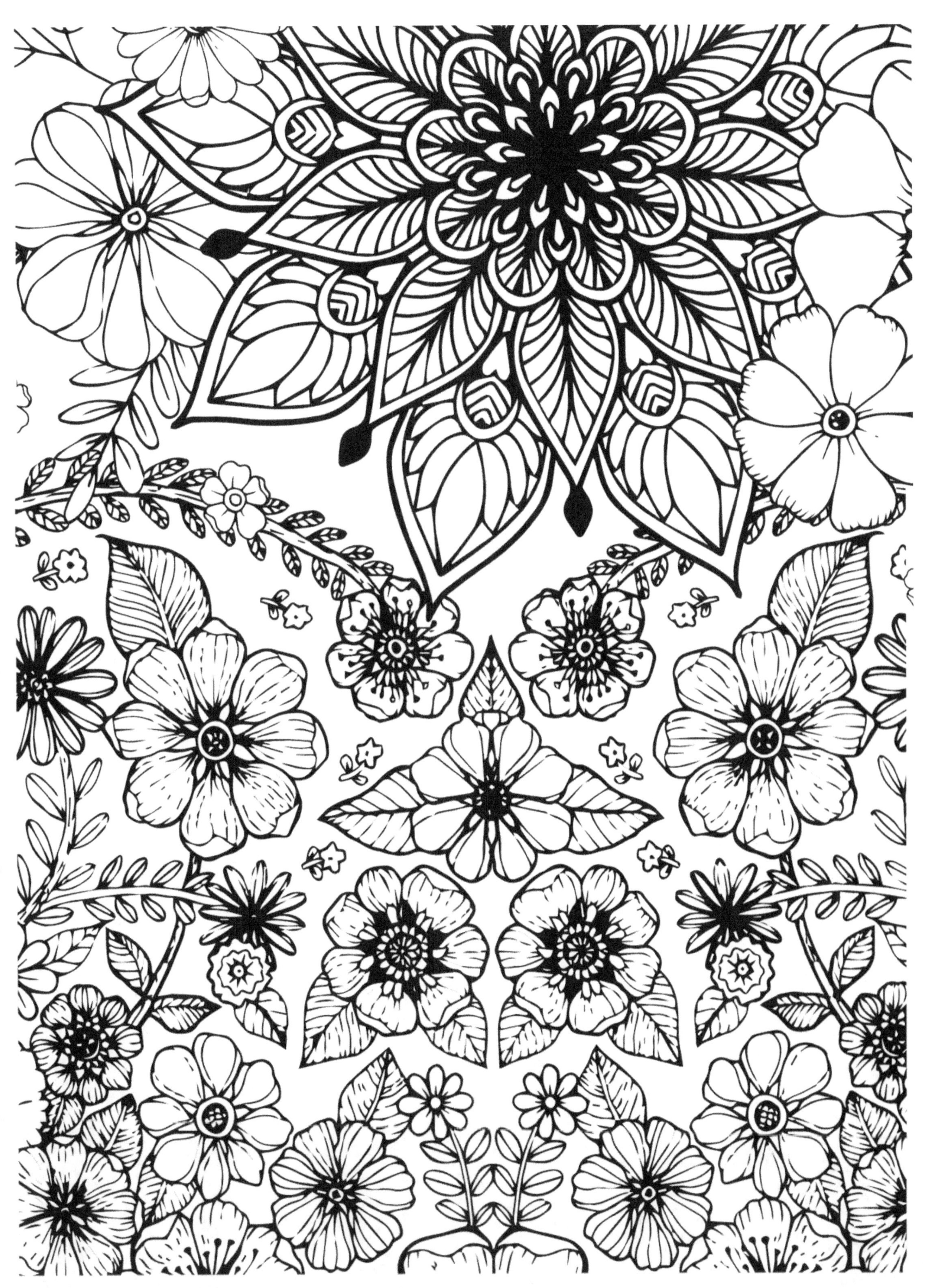

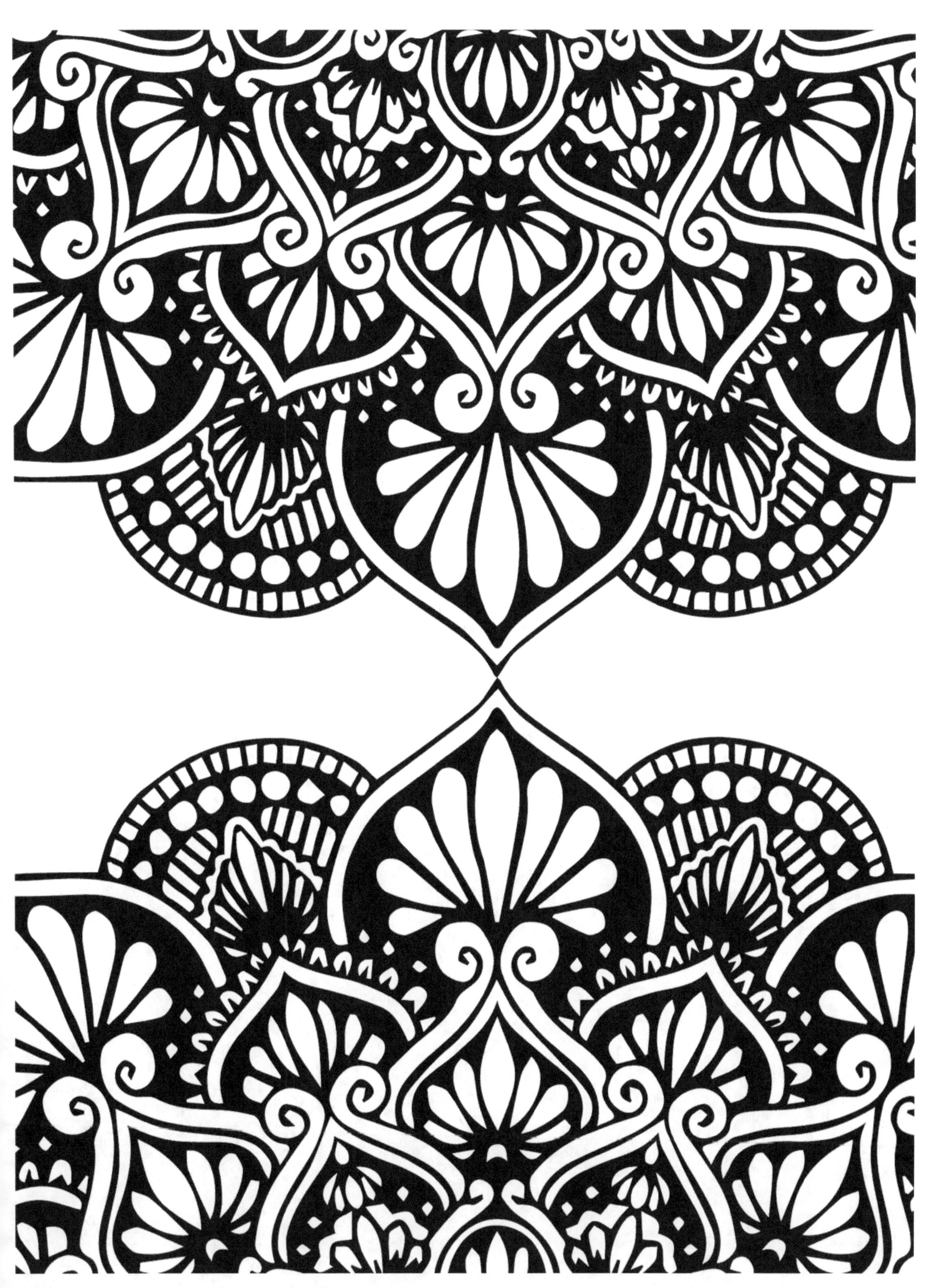

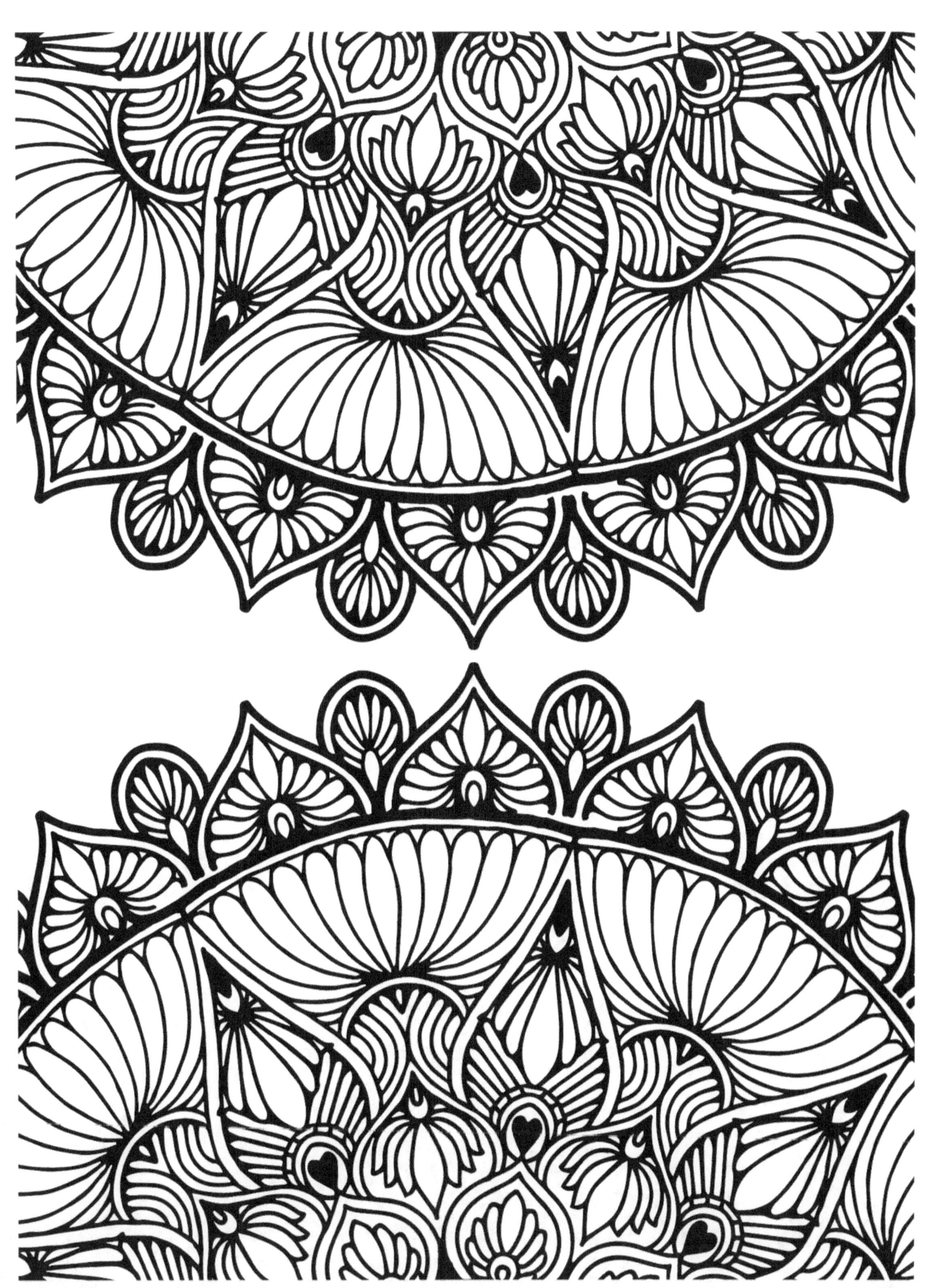

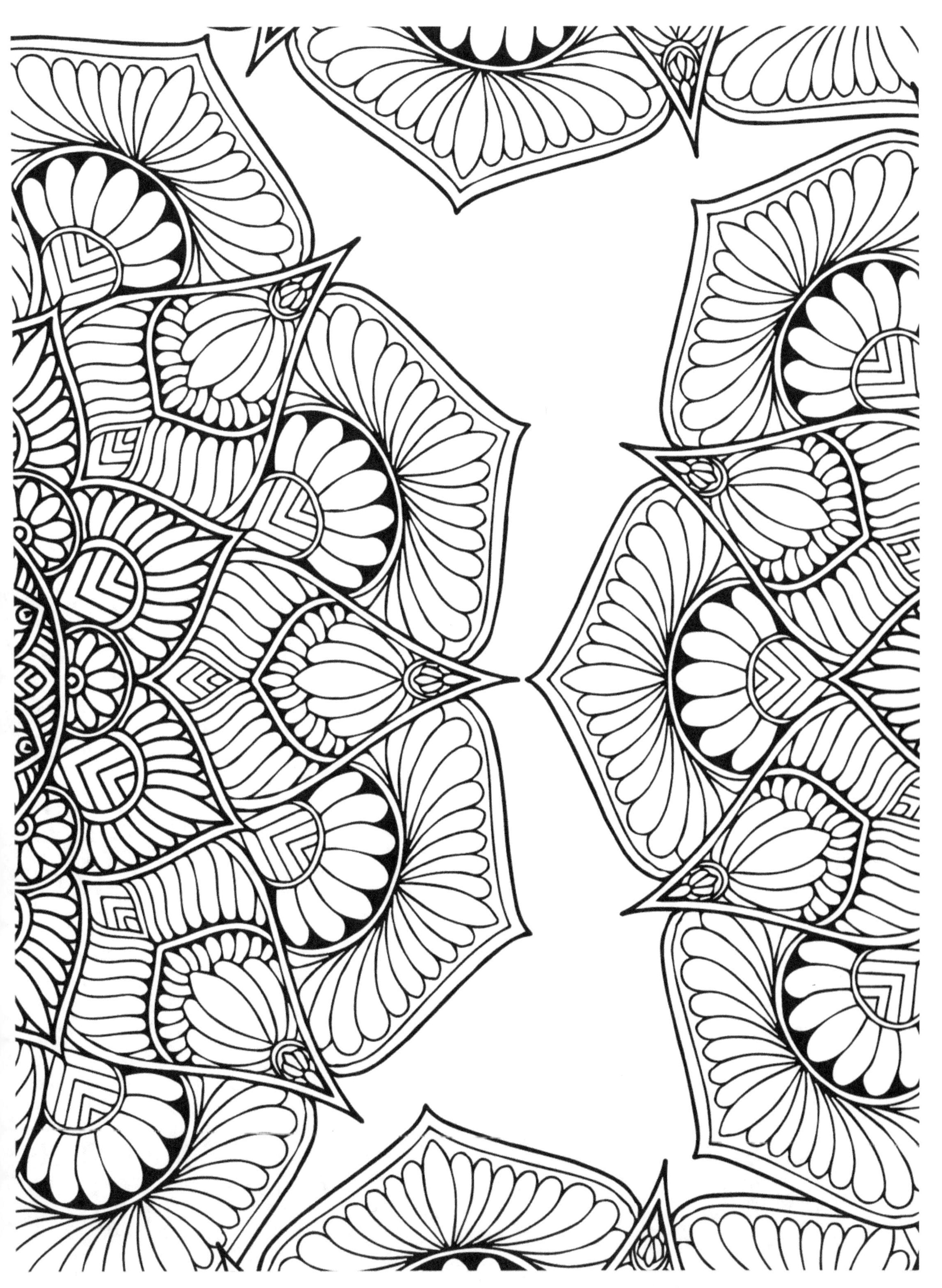

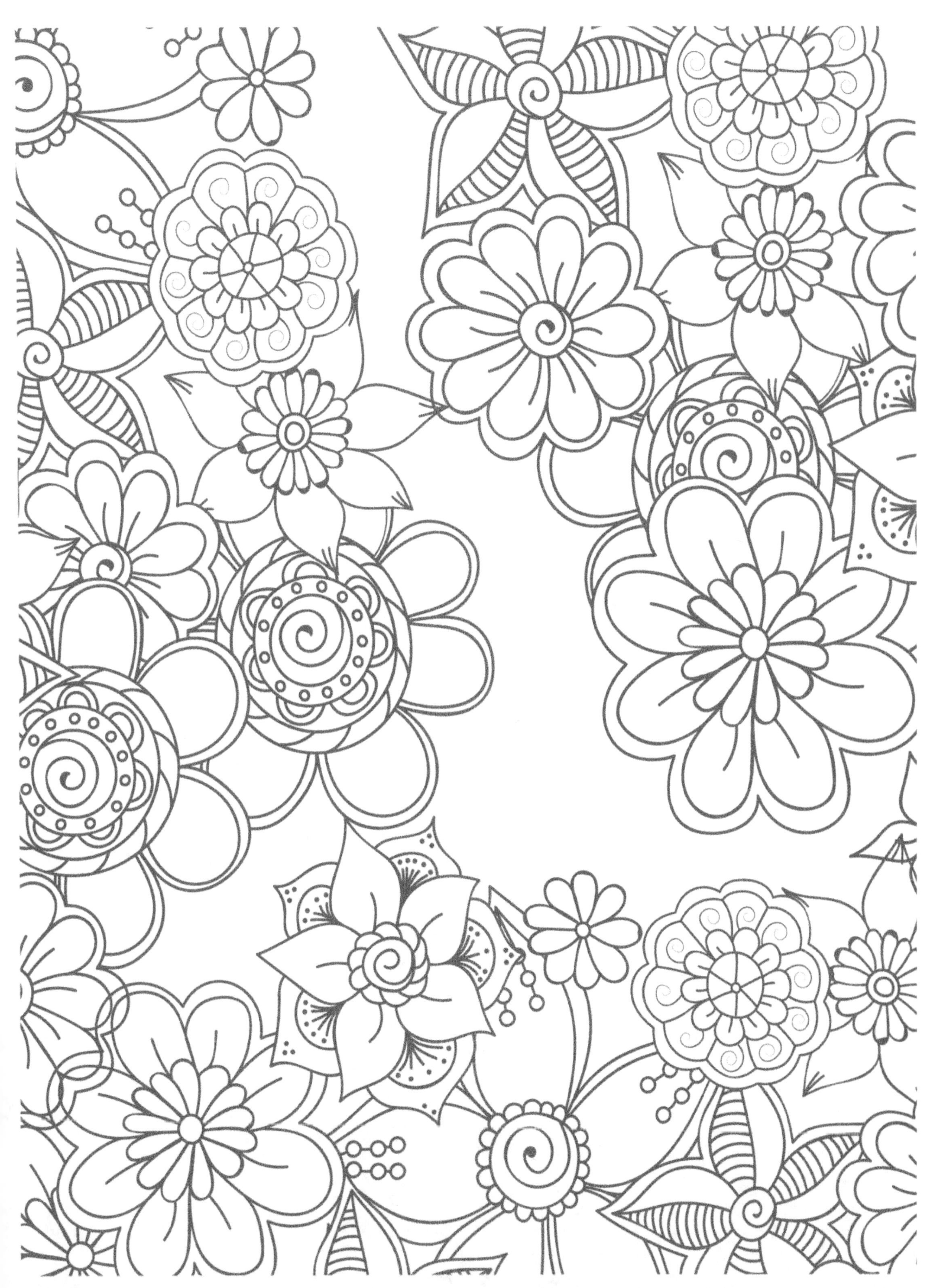

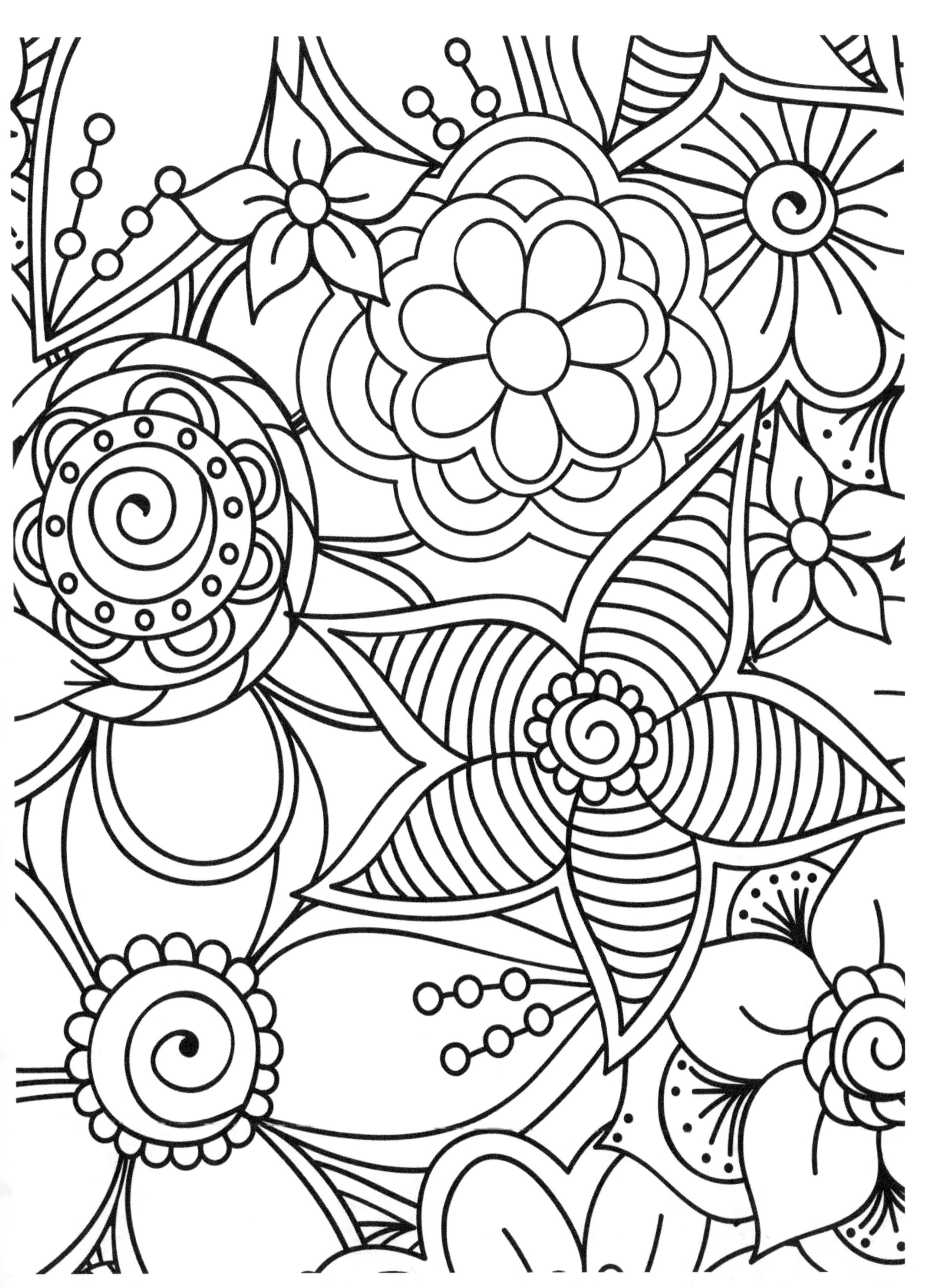

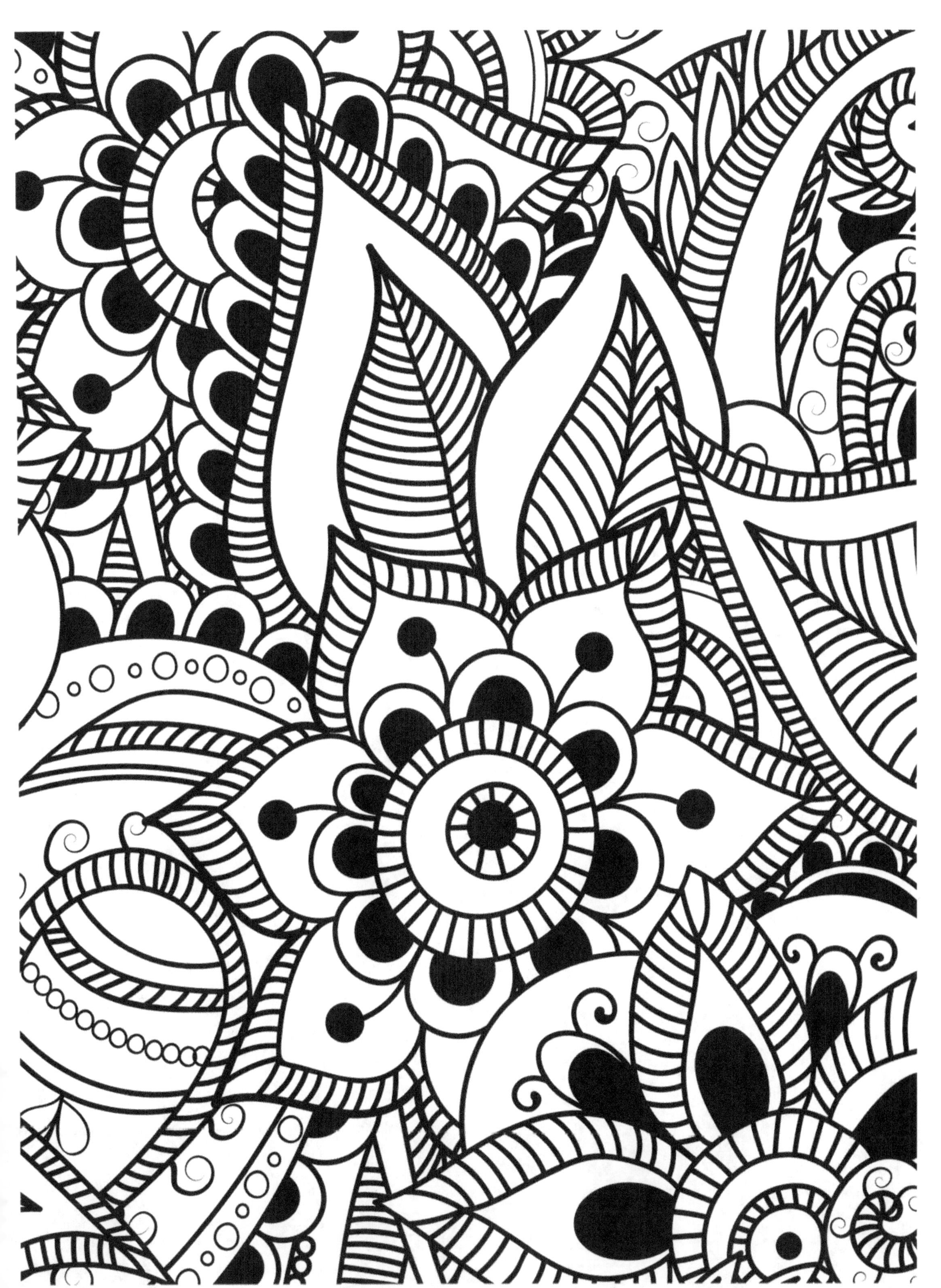

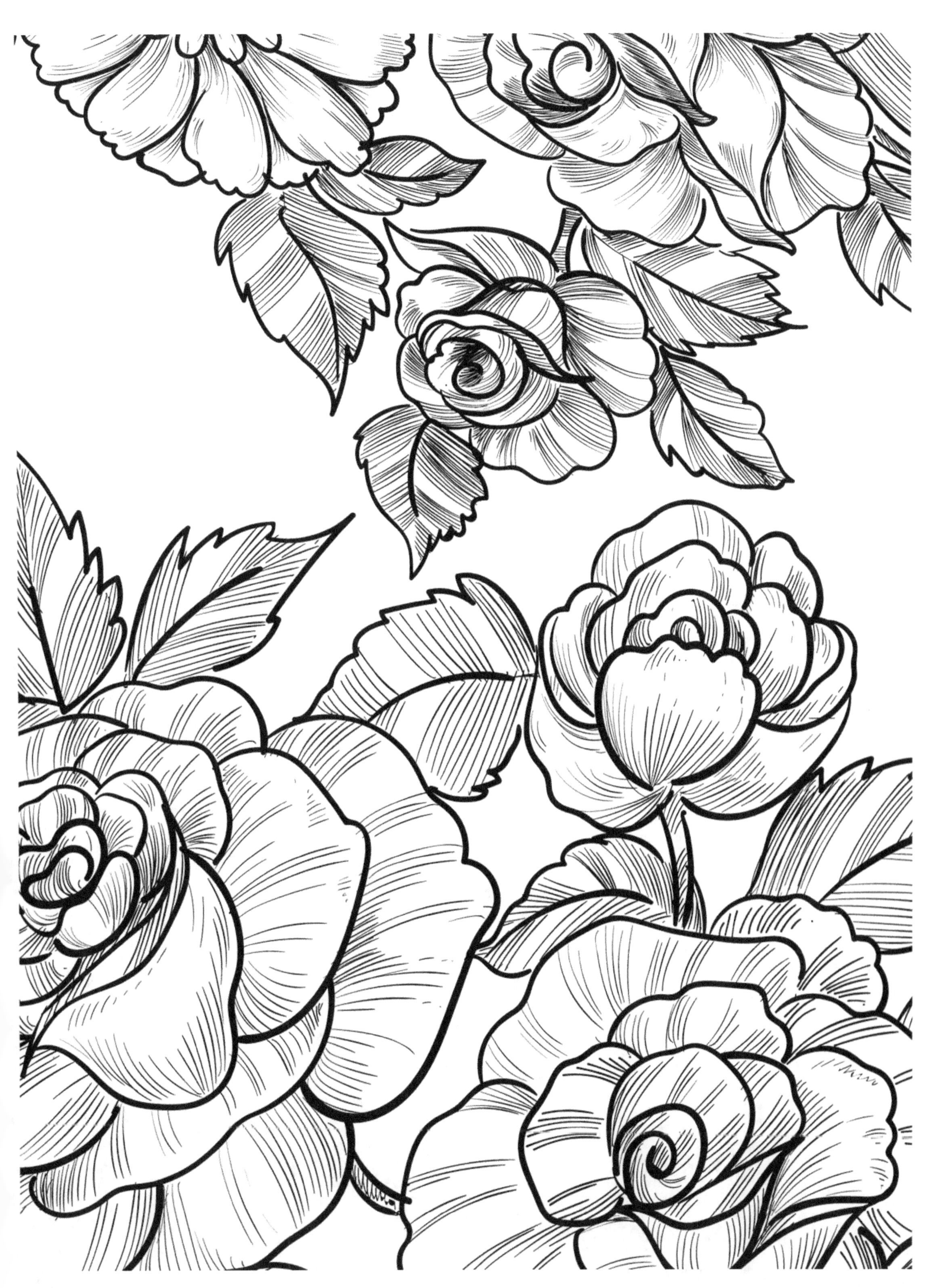

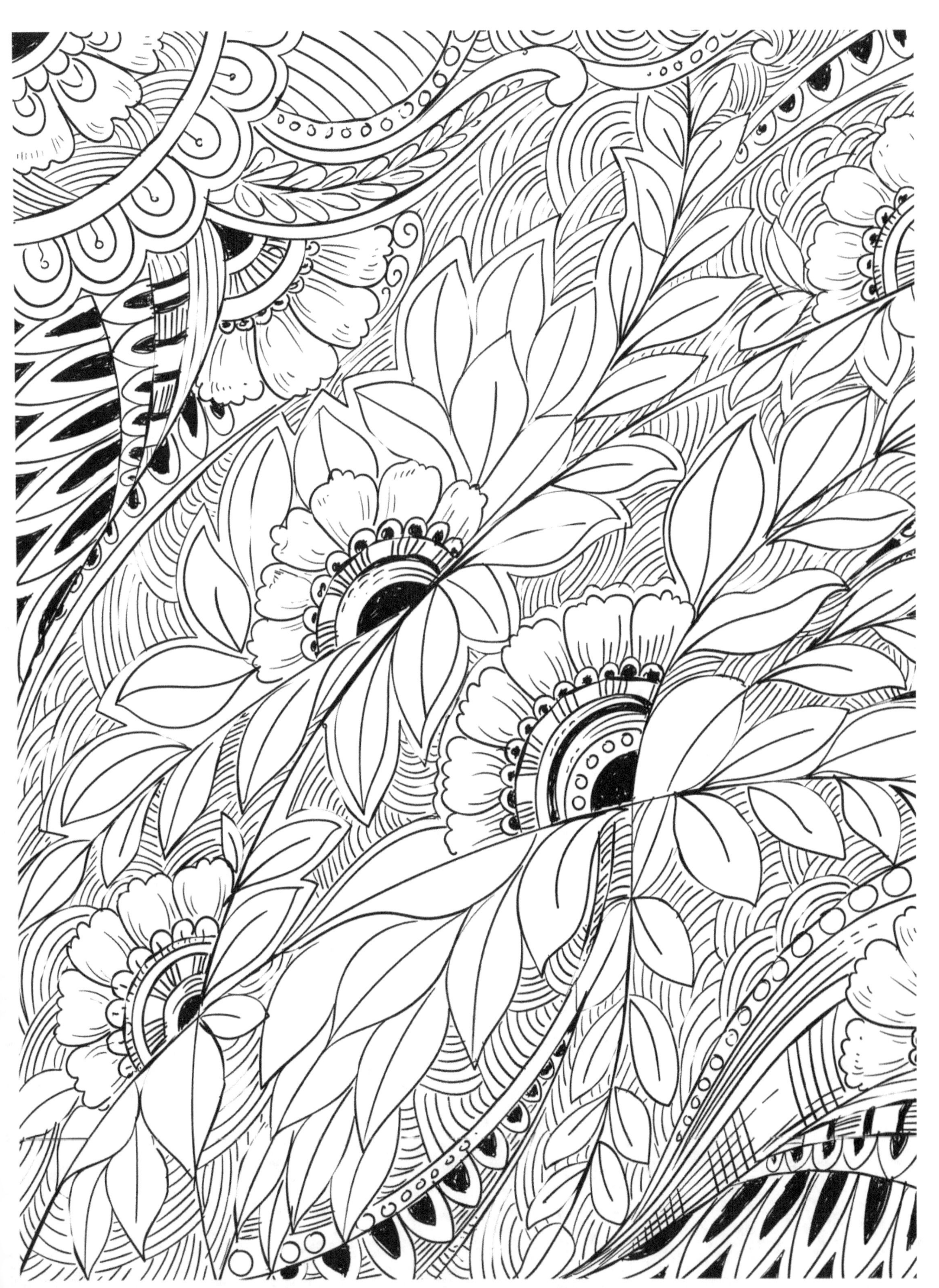

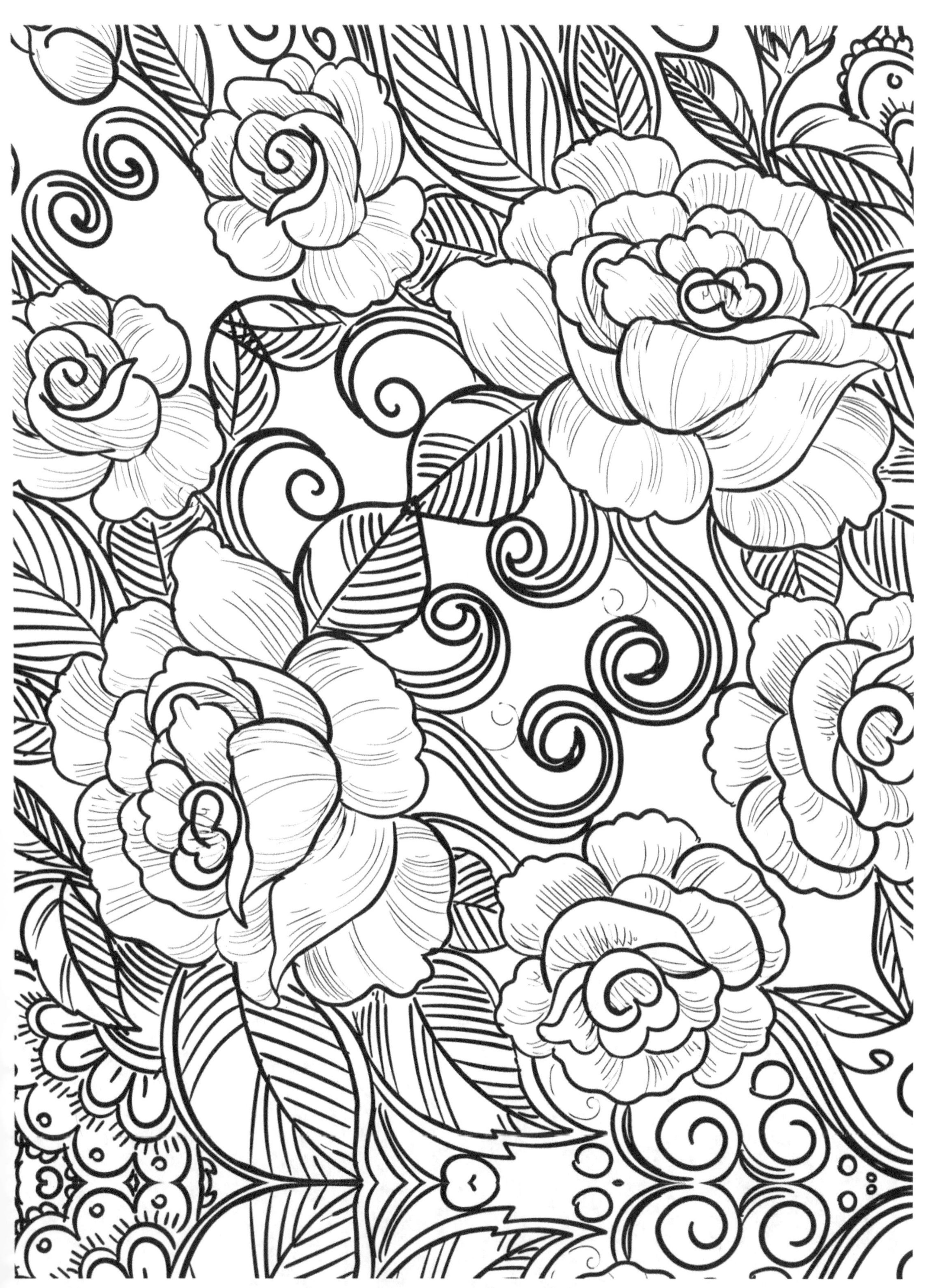